TEXT BOOK OF HERBAL DRUG TECHNOLOGY

[According to latest syllabus of B Pharm - VI semester of Pharmacy Council of India]

Dr. Abhishek Banke
Associate Professor
SIRTS - Pharmacy
Near Isro, Ayodhya Nagar, Bhopal (M. P.)

Dr. Jyoti Nanda Sharma
Assistant Professor
School of Pharmaceutical sciences
C.S.J.M. University,
Kanpur (U. P.)

Dr. Sangita H. Shukla
Principal
Indubhai Patel College of Pharmacy & Research Centre, Ipcowala Education Campus,
Petlad – Khambhat Road, Dharmaj, Dist. Anand (Gujarat)

Ravindra Goswami
Head & Assistant Professor
Department of Botany,
Seth G.B. Podar College,
Rambilad Podar Road, Nawalgarh
(Rajasthan)

Dr. Biswa Mohan Sahoo
Professor
School of Pharmacy and Life Sciences,
Centurion University of Technology & Management,
Bhubaneswar, Khurda (Odisha)

TEXT BOOK OF HERBAL DRUG TECHNOLOGY

First Edition 2024

Published by:

NOTION PRESS

Publisher and distributor

Head Office: Notion press Media Pvt. Ltd.

7, Red cross Road,

Egmore, Chennai,Tamil Nadu 60008

TEXT BOOK OF HERBAL DRUG TECHNOLOGY

NOTION PRESS

PREFACE

The authors feel great pleasure in presenting the first edition of the book "**Text Book of Herbal Drug Technology**" for graduate and post graduate students. The present book on **Text Book of Herbal Drug Technology** has been written according to the syllabus of B. Pharm - VI semester of Pharmacy Council of India and covers full course of the subject.

THE SALIENT FEATURES OF THE BOOK ARE: -

- *Easy to understand style of writing* which makes the book a self-study material.
- *Each new concept has been introduced through day-today problem of interest* to the students which makes the subject matter interesting.
- *The language of the book, on the whole, is lucid and easy to understand.*
- Wherever needed *neatly labeled figures have been drawn.*

The authors hope that the students, teachers and other readers will find the book interesting and to the point covering the course. We hope that the students will receive the book warmly.

I wish to express my sincere thanks to management of M SIRTS-Pharmacy, School of Pharmaceutical sciences, C.S.J.M. University, Indubhai Patel College of Pharmacy & Research Centre, Department of Botany, Seth G.B. Podar College and School of Pharmacy and Life Sciences, Centurion University of Technology & Management, for his heartiest blessing during writing of book.

Every effort is made to keep the book error free. The author will gratefully acknowledge the suggestions to improve the book to make it more useful.

Wishing our readers success in examination and life ahead. The authors feel that their efforts will be fully rewarded if the book serves the purpose for which it is written.

TEXT BOOK OF HERBAL DRUG TECHNOLOGY

CONTENT

CHAPTER - 1

HERBS

Herbs are plants or plant parts that are used for culinary, medicinal, aromatic, or sometimes even spiritual purposes. They are typically valued for their flavor, fragrance, or potential health benefits. Here are some common categories and uses of herbs:

1. **Culinary Herbs:** Culinary herbs are used to flavor food and enhance the taste of various dishes. They can be used fresh or dried. Some popular culinary herbs include basil, oregano, thyme, rosemary, parsley, and mint.
2. **Medicinal Herbs:** Medicinal herbs have been used for centuries for their potential health benefits. They are used in traditional and alternative medicine to treat various ailments. Examples include ginger for digestion, echinacea for immune support, and ginseng for energy.
3. **Aromatic Herbs:** Aromatic herbs are used primarily for their pleasant fragrance. They are often used in perfumes, potpourri, and scented oils. Lavender, chamomile, and rosemary are examples of aromatic herbs.
4. **Herbal Teas:** Many herbs are used to make herbal teas or infusions. These teas are often consumed for their soothing or medicinal properties. Common herbal teas include chamomile tea, peppermint tea, and hibiscus tea.
5. **Herbal Remedies:** Some herbs are used to create natural remedies for various health issues. For example, aloe vera is used topically for skin conditions, and valerian root is used as a natural sleep aid.
6. **Herbal Supplements**: Herbs are also used in the form of dietary supplements, such as capsules, tablets, or tinctures. These supplements can provide concentrated doses of herbal compounds for specific health purposes.

7. **Gardening and Ornamental Herbs:** Some herbs are grown for their ornamental value in gardens. Examples include lavender, rosemary, and thyme, which are not only useful in the kitchen but also add beauty to landscapes.
8. **Spiritual and Ritual Uses:** In various cultures and traditions, certain herbs are used for spiritual or ritual purposes. For example, sage is commonly used in Native American smudging ceremonies.

Definitions:

Herb Definition: A herb, in botanical terms, is a plant with leaves, seeds, or flowers used for flavoring, food, medicine, or fragrance. Herbs are often distinguished from shrubs and trees by their relatively small size, lack of woody stems, and their use primarily in culinary or medicinal applications.

Herbal Medicine: Herbal medicine, also known as phytotherapy or botanical medicine, is a system of healthcare that utilizes plants, plant extracts, and plant-based substances to prevent, alleviate, or treat various medical conditions. It is one of the oldest forms of medicine and has been practiced by various cultures around the world for centuries.

Herbal Medicinal Product: A herbal medicinal product is a finished product, such as a capsule, tablet, ointment, or liquid, that contains one or more herbal substances or preparations made from herbs. These products are intended for therapeutic or medicinal use and are regulated in many countries to ensure their safety, quality, and efficacy.

HERBAL DRUG PREPARATION:

1. **Herbal drug preparations:** It refer to the specific formulations or combinations of herbs and plant-derived substances used for medicinal purposes. These preparations can take various forms, including:

2. **Infusions and Decoctions:** These are prepared by steeping herbs in hot water to extract their active compounds. Teas are a common example.
3. **Tinctures:** Tinctures are alcoholic extracts of herbs and are often more concentrated than teas.
4. **Powders:** Herbs can be dried and ground into a powder, which can be used in capsules or mixed with other ingredients.
5. **Ointments and Creams:** These are topical preparations where herbs are combined with a base like petroleum jelly or a plant-based oil.
6. **Extracts:** Liquid extracts are concentrated solutions of herbal compounds, often preserved with alcohol or glycerin.
7. **Poultices:** A poultice is a soft, moist mass of herbs applied externally to the body.
8. **Herbal Pills and Capsules**: Ground herbs can be encapsulated or compressed into pill form for convenient dosing.

SOURCE OF HERBS

Herbs can be obtained from various sources, depending on whether you are looking for fresh, dried, or processed herbs. Here are some common sources of herbs:

1. **Gardens and Backyards:** Many people grow their own herbs in gardens or pots at home. This is an excellent way to have a fresh and readily available supply of herbs for culinary or medicinal purposes.
2. **Grocery Stores and Supermarkets:** Fresh herbs like basil, cilantro, parsley, and mint are often available in the produce section of grocery stores. Dried herbs can also be found in the spice aisle.

3. **Farmers' Markets:** Local farmers' markets often feature fresh herbs that are in season. These herbs are typically grown locally and can be of high quality.
4. **Specialty Herb Stores:** Some areas have specialty stores that focus exclusively on herbs and herbal products. These stores may offer a wide variety of fresh and dried herbs, as well as herbal supplements and products.
5. **Online Retailers:** You can purchase herbs and herbal products from a wide range of online retailers. This is a convenient option for finding specific herbs or herbal remedies that may not be readily available locally.
6. **Herbalists and Apothecaries**: Herbalists and traditional apothecaries often sell herbs and herbal preparations. They can also provide guidance on selecting the right herbs for specific purposes.
7. **Wild Harvesting:** Some people gather wild herbs from their natural habitats. However, this should be done with caution and knowledge, as not all wild plants are safe for consumption, and over-harvesting can harm natural ecosystems.
8. **Herb Farms:** There are farms dedicated to growing herbs for commercial purposes. These farms supply fresh herbs to restaurants, stores, and consumers.
9. **Home Drying:** You can harvest fresh herbs from your garden or purchase them and then dry them at home. Drying herbs can help preserve them for long-term use.
10. **Community Gardens:** Some communities have shared gardens or herb gardens where members can harvest herbs for personal use.

SELECTION OF SOURCE OF HERBS:

Selecting the right source for herbs is crucial to ensure their quality, safety, and effectiveness, especially when you plan to use them for culinary or medicinal purposes. Here are some important considerations when choosing a source for herbs:

1. **Reputation and Credibility:** Research the reputation and credibility of the source. Look for reviews and testimonials from other customers. Reputable sources are more likely to provide high-quality herbs.
2. **Certifications and Standards:** Check if the source adheres to industry standards and certifications. For example, if you're looking for organic herbs, ensure the source is certified organic. Certification organizations vary by country but may include USDA Organic, EU Organic, or similar certifications.
3. **Transparency:** Choose a source that is transparent about the origin of their herbs, cultivation methods, and processing practices. Knowing where and how the herbs were grown can provide insights into their quality.
4. **Freshness:** If you're looking for fresh herbs, consider sources that have a reputation for providing the freshest products. Herbs should be vibrant, aromatic, and free from wilting or discoloration.
5. **Dried Herb Quality**: If you need dried herbs, look for herbs that have been properly dried and stored to retain their flavor and potency. Well-dried herbs should not be discolored, moldy, or overly brittle.
6. **Organic vs. Conventional:** Decide whether you prefer organic or conventionally grown herbs. Organic herbs are grown without synthetic pesticides and fertilizers, but they can be more expensive. Conventional herbs may be treated with synthetic chemicals.
7. **Local vs. Imported:** Consider whether you want to source herbs locally or if you're open to imported options. Local herbs may be fresher and have a lower carbon footprint, but imported herbs may offer greater variety.

8. **Sustainability:** If sustainability is important to you, inquire about the source's sustainability practices. Some sources prioritize ethical harvesting and sustainable cultivation methods.
9. **Price and Value:** Compare prices across different sources. While quality is essential, you also want to ensure that the herbs are reasonably priced and provide good value for your needs.
10. **Packaging and Storage:** Examine the packaging of the herbs. They should be stored in airtight containers that protect them from moisture, light, and air, which can degrade their quality over time.
11. **Customer Service:** Evaluate the customer service provided by the source. Are they responsive to inquiries? Do they have a return policy if you're not satisfied with your purchase?
12. **Herb Variety:** Ensure that the source offers the specific herbs you need. Some sources may have a wider variety of herbs than others.
13. **Shipping and Delivery:** Consider the source's shipping and delivery options, especially if you're ordering online. Reliable and efficient shipping can help preserve the freshness of the herbs.
14. **Safety and Testing:** Inquire whether the source conducts quality control testing for contaminants and adulterants. This is particularly important if you plan to use herbs for medicinal purposes.
15. **Recommendations and Referrals:** Seek recommendations from herbalists, healthcare professionals, or friends who use herbs. They may have trusted sources to recommend.

IDENTIFICATION AND AUTHENTICATION OF HERBAL MATERIALS

Identification and authentication of herbal materials are critical processes to ensure the quality, safety, and efficacy of herbal products, especially in the context of herbal medicine, dietary supplements, and the herbal industry. Proper identification and authentication help verify the identity of the plant species and ensure that the herbs are free from adulteration, contamination, or mislabeling. Here's a detailed discussion on the methods and considerations for identifying and authenticating herbal materials:

1. **Macroscopic Examination:**
   a. **Visual Inspection:** One of the simplest methods is to visually examine the physical characteristics of the herb, including color, size, shape, texture, and the presence of distinctive features like leaves, stems, flowers, or roots.
   b. **Microscopy:** Microscopic analysis involves examining the cellular structure of the plant under a microscope. Specific cell types, such as trichomes, stomata, and glandular hairs, can provide clues to the plant's identity.
2. **Organoleptic Evaluation:** This involves assessing the taste, smell, and texture of the herb. Different species of plants often have distinct sensory characteristics that can help with identification.
3. **Chemical Analysis:**
   a. **Thin-Layer Chromatography (TLC):** TLC is a technique that separates chemical compounds in a sample based on their movement through a thin layer of a specialized material. It can help identify characteristic compounds in herbs.
   b. **High-Performance Liquid Chromatography (HPLC):** HPLC is used to quantify specific chemical constituents in herbs and compare them to reference standards.
   c. **Gas Chromatography-Mass Spectrometry (GC-MS):** GC-MS can be used to analyze volatile compounds in herbs, aiding in identification.

d. **Nuclear Magnetic Resonance (NMR):** NMR spectroscopy can provide detailed information about the chemical composition of herbal materials.

4. **DNA Barcoding:** DNA barcoding involves sequencing a specific region of the herb's DNA, such as the chloroplast or mitochondrial DNA, and comparing it to known DNA sequences in a database. This method is highly accurate for species identification.
5. **Thin-Layer Chromatography (TLC):** This is a rapid and cost-effective method for fingerprinting herbal materials based on their chemical constituents. Specific compounds and their relative concentrations can be visualized on a TLC plate.
6. **Histochemical Tests:** These tests involve applying specific reagents to sections of the herb to detect the presence of certain compounds. For example, iodine solution can be used to detect the presence of starch.
7. **Microscopic Authentication:** Cross-sections and transverse sections of plant parts can be examined under a microscope to observe cell types, vascular bundles, and other structural characteristics specific to the plant species.
8. **Reference Standards:** Comparing the herbal material to authenticated reference standards is essential. These standards are well-documented samples of known plant species that serve as benchmarks for comparison.
9. **Expert Knowledge:** Herbalists, botanists, and ethnobotanists with expertise in medicinal plants can provide valuable insights into the identification of herbs. Traditional knowledge and indigenous practices can also be helpful.
10. **Adulteration Testing:** To identify adulterants, herbal materials can be tested for the presence of contaminants, fillers, or other plant species that may have been added to increase bulk or lower costs.

11. **Authentication of Geographic Origin:** Certain herbs are known to have distinct characteristics based on where they are grown. Geographical origin can be an important factor in authentication.
12. **Quality Control Standards:** Regulatory agencies in many countries establish quality control standards and guidelines for the identification and authentication of herbal materials. Compliance with these standards is often required for herbal products.

PROCESSING OF HERBAL RAW MATERIAL

The processing of herbal raw materials is a critical step in the production of various herbal products, including herbal medicines, dietary supplements, cosmetics, and herbal teas. Proper processing helps ensure the quality, safety, and efficacy of the final product. Here's a detailed discussion of the processing steps involved in herbal raw material preparation:

1. **Harvesting:**
    a. The first step in processing herbal raw materials is the harvesting of plant parts, such as leaves, stems, roots, flowers, or fruits, depending on the specific herb and its intended use.
    b. Harvesting is typically done at the appropriate stage of plant growth to ensure maximum potency and quality. Timing can vary depending on the herb and the part of the plant being harvested.
2. **Cleaning and Sorting:**
    a. After harvesting, the herbs are cleaned to remove dirt, debris, insects, and other contaminants. This is usually done by hand or with the help of machines.

b. Sorting involves separating damaged or low-quality plant parts from the healthy ones to ensure that only the best materials are processed further.

3. **Drying:**
   a. Drying is a crucial step in herbal processing as it prevents the growth of mold and bacteria, preserves the active compounds, and reduces the risk of spoilage.
   b. Different herbs may require different drying methods, including air drying, sun drying, oven drying, or freeze-drying. The choice of method depends on factors like the herb's moisture content and sensitivity to heat.
4. **Milling and Grinding:** Once dried, some herbs are ground or milled into a fine powder. This is common for herbs used in teas, capsules, or topical products. The particle size may be controlled to meet specific product requirements.
5. **Extraction:**

   For certain herbal products, extraction is used to obtain active compounds. Common extraction methods include:

   a. **Water Extraction:** Suitable for water-soluble compounds.
   b. **Alcohol Extraction:** Used for extracting a wide range of compounds, including alkaloids and essential oils.
   c. **Supercritical Fluid Extraction:** Utilizes carbon dioxide (CO2) as a solvent for extracting specific compounds.
   d. The choice of extraction method depends on the herb's chemical composition and intended use.
6. **Filtration and Separation:** After extraction, the herbal extract may go through filtration and separation processes to remove solid particles and impurities. Filtration can help clarify the extract and improve its appearance.
7. **Concentration:** In some cases, herbal extracts may be concentrated to increase the potency of active compounds or reduce the volume for easier storage and

transport. Concentration can be achieved through methods like evaporation or distillation.

8. **Formulation and Product Manufacturing:** Herbal raw materials, extracts, or powders are often used as ingredients in various herbal products, including capsules, tablets, tinctures, creams, and teas. Formulation involves blending herbal ingredients with other excipients or additives to create the final product.
9. **Quality Control:** Throughout the processing, various quality control measures are implemented to ensure the identity, purity, and potency of the herbal raw materials. This includes testing for contaminants, such as heavy metals, pesticides, and microbes.
10. **Packaging and Storage:** Herbal products should be packaged in containers that protect them from moisture, light, and air to maintain their quality. Proper labeling with ingredient information, expiration dates, and usage instructions is also important.
11. **Regulatory Compliance:** Herbal processing facilities are often subject to regulatory oversight to ensure compliance with quality and safety standards. Compliance with Good Manufacturing Practices (GMP) is common in the herbal industry
12. **Documentation:** Detailed records should be kept at each stage of processing to trace the source of raw materials, processing conditions, and quality control measures. This documentation is important for quality assurance and regulatory purposes.

Multiple Choice Questions (MCQs)

1. Which of the following herbs is NOT typically used for culinary purposes?

   a. Basil

   b. Oregano

c. Echinacea

d. Mint

2. What is the primary use of aromatic herbs?

a. Flavoring food

b. Medicinal purposes

c. Fragrance

d. Spiritual ceremonies

3. Which herb is commonly used in Native American smudging ceremonies?

a. Basil

b. Lavender

c. Sage

d. Rosemary

4. What does the term 'herb' botanically refer to?

a. A plant with flowers

b. A plant with leaves, seeds, or flowers used for various purposes

c. A plant with woody stems

d. A plant used only for medicinal purposes

5. Which of the following is NOT a form of herbal drug preparation?

a. Infusions

b. Tinctures

c. Distillation

d. Poultices

6. Where can you typically find fresh herbs like basil and mint in a store?

a. Frozen section

b. Dairy section

c. Produce section

d. Meat section

7. Which technique involves sequencing a specific region of the herb's DNA for identification? a. Organoleptic Evaluation

b. HPLC

c. DNA Barcoding

d. TLC

8. Which herb is NOT typically grown for ornamental value in gardens?

a. Lavender

b. Rosemary

c. Ginger

d. Thyme

9. Which method is used to extract volatile compounds in herbs?

a. Water Extraction

b. Gas Chromatography-Mass Spectrometry (GC-MS)

c. HPLC

d. DNA Barcoding

10. What is the purpose of drying herbs during processing?

a. To increase their weight

b. To give them a distinct color

c. To prevent mold growth and bacterial contamination

d. To make them taste better

11. What does the term 'herbal medicine' refer to?

a. Only the use of fresh herbs

b. The use of synthetic herbal products

c. A system of healthcare utilizing plants and plant extracts

d. Products that only smell like herbs

12. Which of the following is NOT a method of processing herbal raw material?

a. Harvesting

b. Cleaning

c. Fermenting

d. Drying

13. What is the main purpose of formulating herbal products?

a. For storage purposes

b. For proper packaging

c. To create the final product for consumption or use

d. To make the herbs look more attractive

14. Which method is NOT used for concentrating herbal extracts?

a. Evaporation

b. Distillation

c. Mixing

d. Supercritical Fluid Extraction

15. Why is packaging important for herbal products?

a. To provide a colorful appearance

b. To protect them from moisture, light, and air

c. Only for marketing purposes

d. To increase their shelf life by 10 years

16. Which herb is used topically for skin conditions?

a. Ginseng

b. Aloe vera

c. Chamomile

d. Sage

17. Which herb is known to be used for immune support?

a. Mint

b. Parsley

c. Echinacea

d. Oregano

18. Where can one get guidance on selecting the right herbs for specific purposes?

   a. Novelists

   b. Musicians

   c. Herbalists and Apothecaries

   d. Mathematicians

19. What is one way to ensure the freshness of herbs?

   a. By checking their color

   b. By checking their price

   c. By checking the brand name

   d. By checking the manufacturing date

20. Which of the following is NOT typically a consideration when selecting a source for herbs? a. Reputation and credibility of the source

   b. Packaging and storage

   c. The design of the store or website

   d. Quality control testing for contaminants

Short Answer Type Questions (Subjective)

1. Define a 'herb' in botanical terms.
2. How is 'herbal medicine' different from 'herbal medicinal product'?
3. What are tinctures?
4. List three common sources of herbs.
5. What is the purpose of using DNA barcoding in the identification of herbs?
6. What is the role of microscopy in the identification of herbal materials?
7. Why is the timing of harvesting crucial in herbal processing?
8. What are the primary reasons for drying herbs?
9. Explain the difference between infusions and decoctions.

10. What are the considerations when choosing between organic and conventionally grown herbs?
11. Describe the process of supercritical fluid extraction.
12. What is the significance of quality control in herbal processing?
13. Why is it important to package herbal products in airtight containers?
14. How does the organoleptic evaluation aid in the identification of herbs?
15. What are the potential risks of wild harvesting herbs?
16. Why is it important to be cautious about the geographical origin of herbs?
17. Define the term 'adulteration' in the context of herbs.
18. How does Thin-Layer Chromatography (TLC) aid in the identification of herbal materials?
19. What is the role of regulatory compliance in herbal processing?
20. Why is proper labeling important for herbal products?

Long Answer Type Questions (Subjective)

1. Describe the importance of identification and authentication of herbal materials in the context of the herbal industry.
2. Explain the various steps involved in the processing of herbal raw material, from harvesting to packaging.
3. Discuss the significance of quality control and regulatory compliance in the production of herbal products.
4. Describe the various methods used for extracting active compounds from herbs and their relevance in herbal processing.
5. Explain the considerations one should keep in mind when selecting a source for herbs and why each consideration is important.
6. Discuss the role of traditional knowledge and indigenous practices in the identification and use of herbs.

7. Describe the potential risks and benefits of wild harvesting herbs and the importance of sustainable and ethical harvesting.
8. Explain how different drying methods can impact the quality and potency of herbs.
9. Discuss the challenges associated with ensuring the authenticity and purity of herbal products in the global market.
10. Describe the significance of DNA barcoding and other advanced techniques in the accurate identification of herbal species.

Answer Key for Multiple Choice Questions:

1. c. Echinacea
2. c. Fragrance
3. c. Sage
4. b. A plant with leaves, seeds, or flowers used for various purposes
5. c. Distillation
6. c. Produce section
7. c. DNA Barcoding
8. c. Ginger
9. b. Gas Chromatography-Mass Spectrometry (GC-MS)
10. c. To prevent mold growth and bacterial contamination
11. c. A system of healthcare utilizing plants and plant extracts
12. c. Fermenting
13. c. To create the final product for consumption or use
14. c. Mixing
15. b. To protect them from moisture, light, and air
16. b. Aloe vera
17. c. Echinacea
18. c. Herbalists and Apothecaries

19.a. By checking their color

20.c. The design of the store or website.

CHAPTER - 2

BIODYNAMIC AGRICULTURE

Biodynamic agriculture is an approach to farming that is often described as a holistic, sustainable, and spiritually oriented method of farming. It goes beyond organic farming by emphasizing the interconnectedness of all aspects of farming and seeks to create a balanced and self-sustaining ecosystem within the farm. Biodynamic agriculture was first developed in the early 20th century by Austrian philosopher and scientist Rudolf Steiner, and it has gained recognition as a distinct agricultural approach with its own set of principles and practices. Here are the key principles and practices of biodynamic agriculture:

1. **Holistic Approach:** Biodynamic farming views the farm as a living organism, with all its components (soil, plants, animals, and humans) interconnected and interdependent. It strives to achieve a harmonious balance within this living system.
2. **Biodiversity:** Biodynamic farms emphasize the importance of biodiversity by growing a variety of crops and raising different types of animals. Crop rotation and companion planting are common practices to enhance diversity and reduce the risk of pests and diseases.
3. **Composting:** Composting is central to biodynamic agriculture. Farmers create their compost using a specific method called "biodynamic composting." This compost is rich in organic matter and microbial life, which helps improve soil structure and fertility.
4. **Lunar and Cosmic Rhythms:** Biodynamic farmers follow a planting calendar based on lunar and cosmic rhythms. Planting, cultivating, and harvesting are

timed according to the phases of the moon and celestial influences believed to affect plant growth.

5. **Preparation 500 and 501:** Biodynamic farming involves the use of specific herbal and mineral preparations. Preparation 500 involves burying cow horns filled with manure in the ground during the fall and winter, while Preparation 501 is a spray made from ground quartz crystals stirred into water and sprayed on fields during specific celestial alignments.
6. **Closed Farming System:** Biodynamic farms aim to be self-sustaining and reduce reliance on external inputs. This includes producing their compost, seeds, and animal feed on-site whenever possible.
7. **Livestock Integration:** Biodynamic farms often integrate animals into the farming system. Animals contribute to nutrient cycling through manure production and can also help control pests.
8. **Minimal Use of Chemicals:** Biodynamic farming discourages the use of synthetic chemicals, including pesticides and herbicides. Instead, natural pest and disease management practices are employed.
9. **Soil Health:** Soil health is of utmost importance in biodynamic agriculture. Practices like cover cropping and green manure are used to improve soil fertility and structure.
10. **Spiritual and Ethical Considerations**: Biodynamic farming incorporates spiritual and ethical elements, such as a reverence for nature and a commitment to ethical treatment of animals. It often places a strong emphasis on the farmer's relationship with the land.
11. **Certification:** Biodynamic farms can seek certification from organizations like Demeter International, which sets the standards for biodynamic agriculture. Demeter-certified products are recognized worldwide as biodynamic.

GOOD AGRICULTURAL PRACTICES IN CULTIVATION OF MEDICINAL PLANTS INCLUDING ORGANIC FARMING

Good Agricultural Practices (GAP) are essential guidelines and principles that ensure the sustainable cultivation of medicinal plants while maintaining their quality, safety, and efficacy. GAP for medicinal plant cultivation encompasses various aspects, and when applied alongside organic farming practices, it emphasizes sustainability, environmental stewardship, and health-conscious production.

Good Agricultural Practices (GAP) for the cultivation of medicinal plants are essential to ensure the quality, safety, and sustainability of these valuable botanical resources. Following GAP principles helps maintain the efficacy of medicinal plants while minimizing environmental impact and ensuring product safety.

Here, we will discuss in detail the key components of Good Agricultural Practices, particularly in the context of cultivating medicinal plants and how they relate to organic farming:

1. **Site Selection and Soil Management:**
    a. **Site Selection:** Choose a suitable location with appropriate soil, climate, and elevation for the specific medicinal plants. Consider factors like sunlight, drainage, and proximity to water sources.
    b. **Soil Management:** Implement soil conservation practices, maintain soil fertility through organic matter (compost, green manure), and avoid the use of synthetic chemicals.
2. **Seed and Plant Material Selection:**
    a. Use high-quality seeds or plant materials from reputable sources. Ensure that the genetic identity of the plants is known, and they are disease-free.
3. **Crop Rotation and Diversification:**

a. Implement crop rotation and diversification to prevent soil depletion and minimize the risk of pests and diseases. This is especially important in organic farming.

4. **Water Management:**
   a. Efficiently manage water resources through practices like drip irrigation or rainwater harvesting to minimize water wastage and ensure consistent moisture for medicinal plants.
5. **Integrated Pest Management (IPM):**
   a. Implement IPM strategies to control pests and diseases using natural methods such as beneficial insects, companion planting, and biopesticides, reducing reliance on synthetic chemicals.
6. **Weed Management:**
   a. Use organic weed control methods such as mulching, manual weeding, or mechanical weeders to suppress weed growth without chemical herbicides.
7. **Fertilization:**
   a. Apply organic fertilizers such as compost, manure, and organic amendments to enhance soil fertility and provide essential nutrients to medicinal plants.
8. **Harvesting and Post-Harvest Handling:**
   a. Harvest medicinal plants at the appropriate stage of growth, considering factors like phenological stage and environmental conditions. Handle harvested material with care to minimize damage.
   b. Implement proper drying techniques (e.g., shade drying, air drying) to preserve the quality and potency of the medicinal plants.
9. **Record Keeping and Traceability:**
   a. Maintain detailed records of cultivation practices, including planting dates, inputs used, and harvest dates. This helps in traceability and quality control.

10. Quality Control and Testing:

a. Regularly test and assess the quality of the medicinal plants for active compounds and contaminants. This is crucial for ensuring the safety and efficacy of herbal products.

11. Biodiversity Conservation:

a. Encourage biodiversity on the farm by planting native species, preserving natural habitats, and avoiding monoculture practices. Biodiversity can enhance ecosystem resilience and support beneficial organisms.

12. Organic Certification:

a. Seek organic certification from relevant authorities or certifying bodies to ensure compliance with organic farming standards. Organic certification often aligns with many GAP principles.

13. Ethical Considerations:

a. Consider ethical and cultural aspects of medicinal plant cultivation, including fair labor practices, respect for local communities, and indigenous knowledge.

14. Market Access and Fair Trade:

a. Establish fair trade relationships with buyers to ensure equitable compensation for farmers and promote sustainable markets for medicinal plant products.

15. Continual Learning and Improvement:

a. Stay updated with the latest research and best practices in medicinal plant cultivation, organic farming, and sustainable agriculture. Continually assess and improve your farming methods.

PEST AND PEST MANAGEMENT IN MEDICINAL PLANTS

Pests can pose a significant threat to the cultivation of medicinal plants, as they can damage the plants, reduce yields, and compromise the quality of the medicinal compounds. Effective pest management is essential to protect medicinal plant crops while minimizing the use of synthetic pesticides, which can negatively impact the environment and the quality of the final product. Here's an overview of common pests in medicinal plant cultivation and pest management strategies:

Common Pests in Medicinal Plant Cultivation:

1. **Insects:**
    a. Aphids, thrips, whiteflies, and leafhoppers can feed on plant sap and transmit diseases.
    b. Caterpillars, such as cabbage loopers and armyworms, can defoliate plants.
    c. Beetles, including flea beetles, can damage leaves and stems.
2. **Diseases:**
    a. Fungal diseases like powdery mildew, downy mildew, and various rusts can affect medicinal plants.
    b. Bacterial and viral diseases can also pose threats.
3. **Weeds:**
    a. Weeds compete with medicinal plants for nutrients, water, and sunlight.

Pest Management Strategies:

1. **Integrated Pest Management (IPM):**
    a. IPM is a holistic approach that combines various strategies to manage pests effectively while minimizing harm to the environment.

b. It involves monitoring pest populations, using biological controls (predators and parasites), implementing cultural practices, and, as a last resort, using pesticides judiciously.

2. **Cultural Practices:**
   a. Crop rotation can help break the life cycles of pests and diseases.
   b. Interplanting or companion planting with insect-repelling herbs or flowers can deter some pests.
   c. Proper spacing and pruning can improve air circulation and reduce disease pressure.
3. **Biological Controls:**
   a. Encourage natural predators and parasites that feed on pests. For example, ladybugs, lacewings, and parasitoid wasps can help control aphids and caterpillars.
   b. Release beneficial nematodes to control soil-dwelling pests.
4. **Mechanical Control:**
   a. Hand-picking and physically removing pests, such as caterpillars or beetles, can be effective for small-scale cultivation.
   b. Using row covers or netting can prevent insects from reaching plants.
5. **Traps and Barriers:**
   a. Sticky traps or pheromone traps can capture flying insects.
   b. Physical barriers like floating row covers can protect plants from pest damage.
6. **Organic Pesticides:**
   a. If chemical intervention is necessary, consider using organic and botanical pesticides. These are generally less harmful to the environment and have fewer residues.

b. Neem oil, insecticidal soap, and pyrethrin-based products are examples of organic options.

7. **Cultural Practices for Disease Management:**
   a. Proper sanitation, including removing and disposing of infected plant material, can reduce disease spread.
   b. Using disease-resistant plant varieties when available is a preventive measure.
8. **Biological Fungicides:**
   a. Some biological fungicides, such as those containing beneficial microbes like Bacillus subtilis, can help manage fungal diseases.
9. **Organic Amendments:**
   a. Organic soil amendments like compost can enhance soil health and disease resistance in plants.
10. **Monitoring:**
    a. Regularly inspect plants for signs of pests and diseases.
    b. Implement thresholds for action, where pest populations are controlled when they reach a certain level but not before.
11. **Education and Training:**
    a. Equip yourself and your team with knowledge about pest identification, life cycles, and control methods.

BIOPESTICIDES

Biopesticides are a class of pesticides derived from natural sources, including microorganisms, plants, and certain minerals. Unlike synthetic chemical pesticides, biopesticides are typically less harmful to the environment, non-toxic to humans and non-target organisms when used correctly, and they often have specific modes of action that target pests while sparing beneficial insects and other organisms. Here's a detailed overview of biopesticides:

Types of Biopesticides:

1. **Microbial Biopesticides:**
   a. **Bacteria:** Certain strains of bacteria, such as Bacillus thuringiensis (Bt), produce toxins that are toxic to specific insect pests when ingested. These toxins are used as biopesticides.
   b. **Fungi:** Entomopathogenic fungi like Beauveria bassiana and Metarhizium spp. infect and kill insects. Mycoinsecticides are formulations of these fungi used for pest control.
   c. **Viruses:** Some insect-specific viruses, known as baculoviruses, are used as biopesticides. These viruses infect and kill insect pests, particularly caterpillars and larvae.
2. **Plant-Incorporated Protectants (PIPs):** Certain genetically modified (GM) crops, such as Bt cotton and Bt corn, produce proteins derived from Bt bacteria that are toxic to specific insect pests. These crops are considered biopesticides because they use biological agents (Bt proteins) for pest control.
3. **Botanical Biopesticides:**
   a. Derived from plants, botanical biopesticides use natural compounds or extracts with pesticidal properties. Examples include neem oil, pyrethrum (from chrysanthemum flowers), and rotenone (from the roots of certain plants).
   b. These products can be used to control a range of pests, including insects, mites, and nematodes.
4. **Predatory Insects and Parasitoids**: Certain beneficial insects, such as ladybugs, lacewings, and parasitic wasps, are used as biocontrol agents to prey on or parasitize pest insects.

5. **Biochemical Biopesticides:** Biochemicals are naturally occurring substances that disrupt pest physiology or behavior. For example, insect growth regulators (IGRs) interfere with the molting process of insects, preventing their development to the next stage.

Benefits of Biopesticides:

1. **Environmentally Friendly:** Biopesticides are generally less harmful to the environment because they often target specific pests and have lower persistence in the environment.
2. **Reduced Risk to Non-Target Organisms:** They are less likely to harm beneficial insects, birds, and other non-target organisms.
3. **Low Residue Levels:** Biopesticides often leave lower residues on crops, reducing concerns about chemical residues in food.
4. **Resistance Management:** Their specific modes of action can help delay the development of resistance in pest populations when used correctly.
5. **Compatibility with Integrated Pest Management (IPM):** Biopesticides can be integrated into IPM programs, which combine multiple pest control methods for effective, sustainable management.

Challenges and Considerations:

1. **Effectiveness:** Biopesticides may not be as effective as some synthetic chemical pesticides, and their efficacy can be influenced by environmental factors.
2. **Limited Spectrum:** Many biopesticides are highly specific to certain pests, which means they may not control a broad range of pests.
3. **Short Residual Activity:** Biopesticides often have shorter residual activity than chemical pesticides, requiring more frequent applications.
4. **Regulatory Approval:** Biopesticides must meet regulatory requirements and undergo extensive testing for safety and efficacy before they can be marketed.

Advantages of Biopesticides

1. Environmental Safety:
   - Biodegradable: Biopesticides decompose quickly, reducing the risk of environmental pollution.
   - Non-Toxic to Non-Target Species: They are typically harmless to beneficial insects, birds, and other wildlife, preserving biodiversity.
2. Reduced Resistance:
   - Lower Risk of Resistance Development: Pests are less likely to develop resistance to biopesticides compared to synthetic pesticides because biopesticides often have multiple modes of action.
3. Specificity:
   - Targeted Action: Biopesticides usually target specific pests, reducing the impact on non-target organisms and ecosystems.
4. Health Benefits:
   - Lower Toxicity to Humans: They pose less risk to human health due to their natural origin and lower toxicity.
5. Regulatory Approval:
   - Easier Registration: Biopesticides often face fewer regulatory hurdles and can be approved for use more quickly than synthetic pesticides.
6. Sustainable Agriculture:
   - Support for Organic Farming: Biopesticides are compatible with organic farming practices, promoting sustainable agriculture.

Disadvantages of Biopesticides

1. Limited Spectrum of Activity:

- o Narrow Range: Many biopesticides are specific to certain pests and might not provide broad-spectrum control, requiring the use of multiple products.

2. Variable Efficacy:
   - o Environmental Dependency: Their effectiveness can be influenced by environmental conditions such as temperature, humidity, and sunlight.
3. Shorter Shelf Life:
   - o Stability Issues: Biopesticides often have a shorter shelf life compared to synthetic pesticides, requiring careful storage and handling.
4. Slower Action:
   - o Delayed Effect: They often take longer to suppress pest populations compared to conventional pesticides, which can be a disadvantage in situations requiring immediate action.
5. Higher Cost:
   - o Initial Expense: The initial cost of biopesticides can be higher, and there may be additional costs associated with more frequent applications and integrated pest management strategies.
6. Knowledge and Training:
   - o Need for Expertise: Effective use of biopesticides often requires more knowledge and training in integrated pest management practices.

BIOINSECTICIDES

Bioinsecticides are a category of biopesticides specifically designed to control insect pests. They are derived from natural sources and offer an environmentally friendly and sustainable alternative to synthetic chemical insecticides. Bioinsecticides work by targeting specific insect pests while minimizing harm to non-target organisms and the environment. Here's a detailed overview of bioinsecticides, along with some examples:

Types of Bioinsecticides:

1. **Microbial Bioinsecticides:**
    a. **Bacillus thuringiensis (Bt):** Bt is a naturally occurring bacterium that produces protein crystals toxic to specific insect larvae when ingested. Different strains of Bt target various insect pests, including:
        i. **Bt kurstaki:** Effective against caterpillar pests like cabbage loopers and corn earworms.
        ii. **Bt israelensis:** Targets mosquito and blackfly larvae.
        iii. **Bt aizawai:** Controls caterpillar pests, including gypsy moths.
    b. **Entomopathogenic Fungi:** These fungi infect and kill insects by attaching to their cuticles and invading their bodies. Common examples include:
2. **Beauveria bassiana:** Effective against a broad range of insect pests, including aphids, whiteflies, and beetles.
3. **Metarhizium spp.:** Targets soil-dwelling pests like root damaging insects and termites.
4. **Botanical Bioinsecticides:**
    a. **Neem Oil:** Derived from the neem tree (Azadirachta indica), neem oil contains compounds like azadirachtin that disrupt insect feeding, development, and reproduction. It is effective against a wide range of insect pests, including aphids, caterpillars, and beetles.
    b. **Pyrethrum:** Extracted from chrysanthemum flowers, pyrethrum contains pyrethrins, natural insecticides that target various insects. It is often used

in the form of pyrethrum-based products and is effective against pests like aphids, flies, and mosquitoes.

c. **Rotenone:** Derived from the roots of certain plants, rotenone acts as a stomach poison to insects. It has been used historically but is now less common due to concerns about its environmental impact.

5. **Plant-Incorporated Protectants (PIPs):** Some genetically modified (GM) crops, such as Bt cotton and Bt corn, produce insecticidal proteins derived from Bacillus thuringiensis. These proteins target specific insect pests that feed on the crop.
6. **Predatory Insects and Parasitoids:** Certain beneficial insects, such as ladybugs, lacewings, and parasitic wasps, are used as biocontrol agents to prey on or parasitize insect pests. These natural enemies help keep pest populations in check.
7. **Biochemical Bioinsecticides:**
    a. Biochemical bioinsecticides are naturally occurring compounds or substances that disrupt the physiology or behavior of insect pests.
    b. **Insect Growth Regulators (IGRs):** IGRs interfere with insect development, preventing molting or pupation. They are used to control pests like caterpillars and mosquitoes.

Benefits of Bioinsecticides:

1. **Environmentally Friendly:** Bioinsecticides have minimal environmental impact, as they are generally less harmful to non-target organisms and have lower persistence in the environment.
2. **Target Specificity:** Many bioinsecticides are highly specific to particular insect pests, minimizing harm to beneficial insects and reducing the risk of resistance development.

3. **Reduced Residue Levels:** Bioinsecticides often leave lower residues on crops, making them suitable for integrated pest management (IPM) and reducing concerns about chemical residues in food.

Challenges and Considerations:

1. **Effectiveness:** The efficacy of bioinsecticides can be influenced by environmental conditions, pest populations, and application methods. They may not be as effective as some synthetic chemical insecticides.
2. **Limited Spectrum:** Bioinsecticides are typically designed to control specific pests and may not be effective against a broad range of insects.
3. **Short Residual Activity:** Bioinsecticides often have shorter residual activity than chemical insecticides, requiring more frequent applications.
4. **Regulatory Approval:** Bioinsecticides must mcct rcgulatory requirements and undergo safety and efficacy testing before they can be marketed.

Advantages of Bioinsecticides

1. Environmental Safety:
   - o Biodegradable: Bioinsecticides break down quickly in the environment, reducing the risk of long-term pollution.
   - o Non-Toxic to Non-Target Species: They are generally safe for beneficial insects, birds, and other wildlife, helping to preserve ecosystems.
2. Resistance Management:
   - o Reduced Resistance: Pests are less likely to develop resistance due to the complex modes of action of bioinsecticides, which can involve multiple mechanisms.
3. Specificity:
   - o Targeted Action: Bioinsecticides often target specific pests, minimizing harm to non-target species and beneficial insects such as pollinators.

4. Health Benefits:
    - Lower Human Toxicity: They are typically less toxic to humans, reducing health risks associated with pesticide exposure.
5. Regulatory Ease:
    - Easier Approval: Bioinsecticides generally face fewer regulatory barriers and can often be approved for use more rapidly than synthetic insecticides.
6. Support for Sustainable Practices:
    - Compatibility with Organic Farming: Bioinsecticides can be used in organic farming systems, promoting sustainability and eco-friendly agricultural practices.

Disadvantages of Bioinsecticides

1. Limited Spectrum:
    - Narrow Range of Activity: Many bioinsecticides are effective against specific pests only, which may require the use of multiple products to manage a broader spectrum of pests.
2. Variable Efficacy:
    - Environmental Sensitivity: Their effectiveness can be influenced by environmental conditions such as temperature, humidity, and UV exposure, potentially reducing their reliability.
3. Shorter Shelf Life:
    - Storage Challenges: Bioinsecticides often have a shorter shelf life and may require special storage conditions to maintain their efficacy.
4. Slower Action:

- o Delayed Results: Bioinsecticides might take longer to achieve pest control compared to conventional insecticides, which can be a drawback in urgent situations.

5. Higher Initial Costs:
   - o Economic Considerations: The initial costs of bioinsecticides can be higher, and they may require more frequent applications, potentially increasing overall management costs.
6. Requirement for Knowledge and Training:
   - o Complex Application: Effective use of bioinsecticides often necessitates a good understanding of integrated pest management (IPM) practices and specific knowledge about the pests being targeted.

Multiple Choice Questions (MCQs)

1. Who developed the concept of biodynamic agriculture?
   a. Albert Einstein
   b. Nikola Tesla
   c. Rudolf Steiner
   d. Carl Jung
2. Which of the following is NOT a principle of biodynamic agriculture?
   a. Using synthetic fertilizers
   b. Biodiversity
   c. Lunar and Cosmic Rhythms
   d. Livestock Integration
3. What is the primary purpose of Preparation 501 in biodynamic farming?
   a. Improving soil texture
   b. Spraying on fields during celestial alignments

c. Feeding livestock

d. Protecting plants from frost

4. In Good Agricultural Practices (GAP) for medicinal plants, which factor is important during site selection?

   a. Design of the farmhouse

   b. Soil, climate, and elevation

   c. Proximity to the city

   d. Availability of machinery

5. Which biopesticide is derived from the neem tree?

   a. Rotenone

   b. Pyrethrum

   c. Neem Oil

   d. Bt toxin

6. Which organism is NOT used as a microbial bioinsecticide?

   a. Bacillus thuringiensis

   b. Beauveria bassiana

   c. Escherichia coli

   d. Metarhizium spp.

7. Integrated Pest Management (IPM) combines:

   a. Only chemical methods for pest control

   b. Only biological methods for pest control

   c. Various strategies for effective pest control

   d. Only cultural practices for pest control

8. Which of the following is NOT a benefit of biopesticides?

   a. High persistence in the environment

   b. Environmentally friendly

   c. Reduced risk to non-target organisms

d. Low residue levels

9. Which biodynamic preparation involves burying cow horns filled with manure?

a. Preparation 400

b. Preparation 499

c. Preparation 500

d. Preparation 501

10. Which organization sets standards for biodynamic agriculture?

a. FAO

b. WHO

c. Demeter International

d. USDA

11. Which term refers to a GM crop that produces insecticidal proteins?

a. Bioherbicide

b. Biofungicide

c. Plant-Incorporated Protectant

d. Biopesticide

12. Which of the following is NOT a type of biopesticide?

a. Botanical

b. Microbial

c. Chemical

d. Plant-Incorporated Protectants

13. Biodiversity conservation in GAP emphasizes:

a. Monoculture practices

b. Planting only exotic species

c. Planting native species and avoiding monoculture

d. Removing natural habitats

14. In GAP for medicinal plants, what is a common method for weed management?

a. Using only chemical herbicides

b. Ignoring weed growth

c. Using organic methods like mulching and manual weeding

d. Using fire to burn weeds

15. Which of the following is a focus of biodynamic agriculture?

a. Relying heavily on external inputs

b. Using only synthetic chemicals for pest control

c. Viewing the farm as a living organism

d. Focusing solely on maximizing profit

16. Which insect is beneficial in bioinsecticide applications?

a. Aphids

b. Ladybugs

c. Whiteflies

d. Armyworms

17. Which is a common fungal disease affecting medicinal plants?

a. Common cold

b. Downy mildew

c. Malaria

d. Tuberculosis

18. What do biodynamic farmers use to determine planting, cultivating, and harvesting times?

a. A standard calendar

b. A lunar and cosmic rhythm-based calendar

c. Random selection

d. An almanac

19. Which of the following best describes bioinsecticides?

a. Synthetic chemicals for insect control

b. Natural sources designed to control insect pests

c. General fungicides

d. Soil fertilizers

20. In GAP, what is essential to ensure traceability and quality control?

a. Avoiding record-keeping

b. Keeping detailed records of cultivation practices

c. Relying on memory

d. Documenting only pesticide applications

Short Answer Type Questions (Subjective)

1. Define biodynamic agriculture.
2. What is the significance of composting in biodynamic farming?
3. List two main differences between organic farming and biodynamic farming.
4. Describe Preparation 500 in biodynamic agriculture.
5. What is the importance of biodiversity in Good Agricultural Practices for medicinal plants?
6. Explain the role of Integrated Pest Management in the cultivation of medicinal plants.
7. How do botanical biopesticides differ from microbial biopesticides?
8. Describe the role of Beauveria bassiana in bioinsecticides.
9. How does crop rotation benefit the cultivation of medicinal plants?
10. Why is soil management a crucial component of Good Agricultural Practices?
11. What is the significance of using high-quality seeds in the cultivation of medicinal plants?
12. How do bioinsecticides minimize harm to the environment?
13. What is the role of entomopathogenic fungi in pest management?
14. Describe the benefits of neem oil as a bioinsecticide.

15. Why is site selection crucial in Good Agricultural Practices for medicinal plants?
16. How do biopesticides contribute to resistance management in pest populations?
17. What is the role of predatory insects in bioinsecticide applications?
18. Describe the significance of crop diversification in organic farming.
19. What are the ethical considerations in Good Agricultural Practices for medicinal plants?
20. Why is water management essential in the cultivation of medicinal plants?

Long Answer Type Questions (Subjective)

1. Discuss the principles and practices of biodynamic agriculture and how they differ from conventional farming.
2. Explain the key components of Good Agricultural Practices in the context of cultivating medicinal plants.
3. Describe the various types of biopesticides and their applications in agricultural practices.
4. Discuss the role and significance of Integrated Pest Management in ensuring the sustainable cultivation of medicinal plants.
5. Elaborate on the challenges associated with the use of biopesticides and how they can be addressed.
6. Explain the importance of biodiversity conservation in Good Agricultural Practices and its implications for the environment and agricultural sustainability.
7. Describe the different types of bioinsecticides and their mechanisms of action against insect pests.
8. Discuss the environmental and health benefits of adopting bioinsecticides over synthetic chemical insecticides.

9. Explain the role of microbial bioinsecticides in pest management and their advantages over other types of bioinsecticides.
10. Describe the considerations and challenges in implementing Good Agricultural Practices in the cultivation of medicinal plants.

Answer Key for Multiple Choice Questions

1. c. Rudolf Steiner
2. a. Using synthetic fertilizers
3. b. Spraying on fields during celestial alignments
4. b. Soil, climate, and elevation
5. c. Neem Oil
6. c. Escherichia coli
7. c. Various strategies for effective pest control
8. a. High persistence in the environment
9. c. Preparation 500
10. c. Demeter International
11. c. Plant-Incorporated Protectant
12. c. Chemical
13. c. Planting native species and avoiding monoculture
14. c. Using organic methods like mulching and manual weeding
15. c. Viewing the farm as a living organism
16. b. Ladybugs
17. b. Downy mildew
18. b. A lunar and cosmic rhythm-based calendar
19. b. Natural sources designed to control insect pests
20. b. Keeping detailed records of cultivation practices

CHAPTER - 3

INDIAN SYSTEMS OF MEDICINE

AYURVEDIC SYSTEM OF MEDICINE

INTRODUCTION:

Ayurveda originated in India long back in pre-vedic period. *Rigveda* and *Atharva-veda* (5000 years B.C.), the earliest documented ancient Indian knowledge have references on health and diseases. Ayurveda texts like *Charak Samhita* and *Sushruta Samhita* were documented about 1000 years B.C.

The term *Ayurveda* means 'Science of Life'. It deals elaborately with measures for healthful living during the entire span of life and its various phases. Besides, dealing with principles for maintenance of health, it has also developed a wide range of therapeutic measures to combat illness. These principles of positive health and therapeutic measures relate to physical, mental, social and spiritual welfare of human beings. Thus *Ayurveda* becomes one of the oldest systems of health care dealing with both the preventive and curative aspects of life.

The Ayurveda have eight disciplines:

1. Internal Medicine (Kaya Chikitsa).
2. Pediatrics (Kaumar Bhritya).
3. Psychiatry (Bhoot Vidya).
4. Surgery (Shalya).
5. Otorhinolaryngology and Ophthalmology (Shalakya).
6. Toxicology (Agad Tantra).
7. Geriatrics (Rasayana).
8. Eugenics and aphrodisiacs.

PRINCIPLE OF AYURVEDIC SYSTEM OF MEDICINE:

Body Matrix: Life in Ayurveda is conceived as the union of body, senses, mind and soul. The living man is a conglomeration of three humours (*Vata, Pitta & Kapha*), seven basic tissues (*Rasa, Rakta, Mansa, Meda, Asthi, Majja & Shukra*) and the waste products of the body such as faeces, urine and sweat. Thus the total body matrix comprises of the humours, the tissues and the waste products of the body. The growth and decay of this body matrix and its constituents revolve around food which gets processed into humours, tissues and wastes. Ingestion, digestion, absorption, assimilation and metabolism of food have interplay in health and disease which are significantly affected by psychological mechanisms as well as by bio-fire (Agni).

Panchamahabhutas: The human body is composed of five basic elements (Panchamahabhutas):

1. Earth.
2. Water.
3. Fire.
4. Air
5. Vacuum (ether).

There is a balanced condensation of these elements in different proportions to suit the needs and requirements of different structures and functions of the body matrix and its parts. The growth and development of the body matrix depends on its nutrition, i.e. on food. The food, in turn, is composed of the above five elements, which replenish or nourish the like elements of the body after the action of bio-fire (*Agni*).

Health and Sickness: Health or sickness depends on the presence or absence of a balanced state of the total body matrix including the balance between its different constituents. Both the intrinsic and extrinsic factors can cause disturbance in the natural equilibrium giving rise to disease. This loss of equilibrium can happen by dietary indiscrimination, undesirable habits and non-observance of rules of healthy living. Seasonal abnormalities, improper exercise or erratic application of sense organs and incompatible actions of the body and mind can also result in creating disturbance of the existing normal balance. The treatment consists of restoring the balance of disturbed body-mind matrix through regulating diet, correcting life-routine and behaviour, administration of drugs and resorting to preventive Panchkarma and *Rasayana* therapy.

Diagnosis: In Ayurveda diagnosis is always done of the patient as a whole. The physician takes a careful note of the patient's internal physiological characteristics and mental disposition. He also studies such other factors as the affected bodily tissues, humours, the site at which the disease is located, patient's resistance and vitality, his daily routine, dietary habits, the gravity of clinical conditions, condition of digestion and details of personal, social, economic and environmental situation of the patient. The diagnosis consists of following examinations:

1. Physical examination.
2. Pulse examination
3. Urine examination
4. Examination of tongue and eyes
5. Examination of the faeces
6. Examination of skin and ear.

TREATMENT:

Objectives of Ayurveda:

1. Maintenance and promotion of health.
2. Prevention of disease and cure of sickness.

Normally treatment measures involve use of medicines, specific diet and prescribed activity routine. Use of these three measures is done in two ways. In one approach of treatment the three measures antagonize the disease by counteracting the etiological factors and various manifestations of the disease. In the second approach the same three measures of medicine, diet and activity are targeted to exert effects similar to the etiological factors and manifestations of the disease process. These two types of therapeutic approaches:

1. Vipreeta Treatment.
2. Vipreetarthkari treatments.

For successful administration of a treatment four things are essential. These are:

1. The Physician
2. The medicaments.
3. The nursing personnel.
4. The patient.

Type of Treatment: The treatment of disease are classify as follows:

1. Shodhana therapy (Purification Treatment).
2. Shamana therapy (Palliative treatment).
3. Pathya Vyavastha (Prescription of diet and activity).
4. Nidan Parivarjan (Avoidance of disease causing and aggravating factors).
5. Satvavajaya (Psychotherapy).
6. Rasayana therapy (Use of Immunomodulator and rejuvenation factor).

1. **Shodhana therapy (Purification Treatment):** aims at removal of the causative factors of somatic and psychosomatic diseases. The process involves internal and external purification. The usual practices involved are *Panchkarma* (medically induced Emesis, Purgation, Oil Enema, Decoction enema and Nasal

administration of medicines), Pre-Panchkarma procedures (external and internal oleation and induced sweating). *Panchkarma* treatment focuses on metabolic management. It provides needed purificatory effect, besides conferring therapeutic benefits. This treatment is especially helpful in neurological disorders, musculo-skeletal disease conditions, certain vascular or neuro-vascular states, respiratory disease, metabolic and degenerative disorder.

2. **Shamana therapy (Palliative treatment):** It involves suppression of vitiated humours. The process by which disturbed humour subsides or returns to normal without creating imbalance of other humours is known as shamana. This treatment is achieved by use of appetizers, digestives, exercise and exposure to sun, fresh air etc. in this form of treatment, palliatives and sedatives are used.
3. **Pathya Vyavastha (Prescription of diet and activity):** It comprises indications and contraindications in respect of diet, activity, habits and emotional status. This is done with a view to enhance the effects of therapeutic measures and to impede the pathogenetic processes. Emphasis on do's and don'ts of diet etc is laid with the aim to stimulate Agni and optimize digestion and assimilation of food in order to ensure strength of tissues.
4. **Nidan Parivarjan:** is to avoid the known disease causing factors in diet and lifestyle of the patient. It also encompasses the idea to refrain from precipitating or aggregating factors of the disease.
5. **Satvavajaya (Psychotherapy):** It concerns mainly with the area of mental disturbances. This includes restraining the mind from desires for unwholesome objects and cultivation of courage, memory and concentration. The study of psychology and psychiatry has been developed extensively in *Ayurveda* and has wide range of approaches in the treatment of mental disorder.
6. **Rasayana therapy:** It deals with promotion of strength and vitality. The integrity of body matrix, promotion of memory, intelligence, immunity against

the disease, the preservation of youth, luster and complexion and maintenance of optimum strength of the body and senses are some of the positive benefits credited to this treatment. Prevention of premature bear and tear of body tissues and promotion of total health content of an individual are the roles that Rasayana therapy plays.

Diet and Ayurvedic treatment: In Ayurveda, regulation of diet as therapy has great importance. This is because it considers human body as the product of food. An individual's mental and spiritual development as well as his temperament is influenced by the quality of food consumed by him. Food in human body is transformed first into chyle or *Rasa* and then successive processes involve its conversion into blood, muscle, fat, bone, bone-marrow, reproductive elements and *ojas*. Thus, food is basic to all the metabolic transformations and life activities. Lack of nutrients in food or improper transformation of food lead to a variety of disease conditions

UNANI SYSTEM OF MEDICINE

Unani Medicine is based on the Greece philosophy. According to Basic Principals of Unani the body is made up of the four Basic elements i.e. Earth, Air, Water, Fire which have different Temperaments i.e. Cold, Hot, Wet, Dry. After mixing and interaction of four elements a new compound having new temperament comes into existence i.e. Hot Wet, Hot Dry, Cold Wet, and Cold Dry. The body has the Simple and Compound Organs which got their nourishment through four Humours i.e. Blood, Phlegm, Yellow Bile, Black Bile. The humour also assigned temperament as blood is hot and wet, Phlegm is cold and hot, yellow bile is hot and dry and black bile is cold and dry.

Unani medicine believes in promotion of health, prevention of diseases and cure.

Health of human is based on the six essentials (Asbabe Sitta Zaroorya).

The six essentials are:

1. Atmosphere air.
2. Physical activity and rest.
3. Drinks and food.
4. Sleep and wakefulness.
5. Excretion and retention.
6. Mental activity and rest.

Diagnosis of disease: Diseases are mainly diagnosed with the help of:

1. Pulse (Nabz).
2. Examination of urine and stool.

Treatments: The diseases are treated in as follows:

1. Ilajbil Tadbeer (Regimenal Therapy).
2. Ilajbil Ghiza (Dietotherapy)
3. Ilajbil Dava (Pharmacotherapy).
4. Ilajbil Yad (Surgery).

1. **Ilajbil Tadbeer (Regimenal Therapy):** Some drugless regimens are advised for the treatment of certain ailments i.e. Exercise, Massage, Hamam (Turkish bath), Douches (Cold and Hot) and the regimen for Geriatrics.
2. **Ilajbil Ghiza (Dietotherapy):** Different diets are recommended for the patients of different diseases.
3. **Ilajbil Dava (Pharmacotherapy):** The basic concept of treatment is to correct the cause of the disease that may be abnormal temperament due to:
   (i) Environmental factors.
   (ii) Abnormal humors either due to internal causes or external causes which may be pathogenic micro-organism, through (a)drugs of opposite

temperament to the temperament of the disease that is called Ilaj-bil-zid or (b) drugs of similar temperament of the disease that is called as Ilaj-bil-misl.

The drugs used are mostly of the Plant origin. Some drugs of Animal and Mineral Origin are also used. Patients are treated either by single drugs (crude drugs) or by compound drugs (formulations of single drugs).

SIDDHA SYSTEM OF MEDICINE

INTRODUCTION:

Siddha medicine is practiced in Southern India. The origin of the Tamil language is attributed to the sage Agasthya and the origin of Siddha medicine is also attributed to him. Before the Aryan occupation of the Sind region and the Gangetic plain there existed in the southern India, on the banks of the river Kavery, and Tamirapani, a civilization which was highly organized

1. This civilization has a system of medicine to deal with problems of sanitation and treatment of diseases. This is the Siddha system of medicine. It is possible that in the course of time this system and the one prevalent in the north supplemented and enriched each other. The therapeutics of Siddha medicines consists mainly of the use of metals and minerals whereas in the earlier Ayurveda.
2. There is mention of mercury, sulphur, copper, arsenic and gold used as therapeutic agents.

PRINCIPLE OF SIDDHA SYSTEM OF MEDICINE:

The universe consists of two essential entities, matter and energy. The Siddhas call them Siva (male) and Shakti (female, creation). Matter cannot exist without energy inherent in it and vice versa. The two co-exist and are inseparable.

They are the primordial elements Bhutas, not to be confused with modern chemistry. Their names are *Munn* (solid), *Neer* (fluid), *Thee* (radiance), *Vayu* (gas) and *Aakasam* (ether). These five elements (Bhutas) are present in every substance, but in different proportions. Earth, water, fire, air and ether are manifestations of five elements.

The human being is made up of these five elements, in different combinations. The physiological function in the body is mediated by three substances (dravayas), which are made up of the five elements. They are *Vatham, Pitham,* and *Karpam*. In each and every cell of the body these three *doshas* co-exist and function harmoniously. The tissues are called *dhatus. Vatham* is formed by *Akasa* and *Vayu. Vatham* controls the nervous actions such as movement, sensation, etc. *Pitham* is formed by *Thee* and controls the metabolic activity of the body, digestion, assimilation, warmth, etc. *Kapam* is formed by *Munn* and *Neer* and controls stability. When their equilibrium is upsets disease sets in.

The five elements are:

1. Munn.
2. Neer.
3. Thee.
4. Vayu.
5. Aakasam.

Tridoshas according to Siddha Medicine: The tridoshas are involved in all functions of the body, physical, mental and emotional.

1. **Vatham:**
    a. characteristic is dryness, lightness, coldness & motility
    b. Formed by Aakasam and Vayu, controls the nervous action that constitute movement, activity, sensation, etc. Vatham predominates in the bone.

c. Vatham predominates in first one third of life when activity, growth , sharpness of function of sense, are greater

2. **Pitham:**
   a. heat, mover of the nervous force of the body
   b. Formed by Thee, controls the metabolic activity of the body, digestion, warmth, lustre, intellect, assimilation,etc. Pitham predominates in the tissue blood.
   c. Pitham predominates in the second one third of life
3. **Karpam:**
   a. smoothness, firmness, viscidity, heaviness
   b. Formed by munn and Neer, controls the stability of the body such as strength, potency, smooths working of joints. Karpam predominates in other tissues.
   c. Karpam predominates in the last one third of life. Diminishing activity of various organs and limbs

The seven dhatus are:

1. Rasa (lymph).
2. Kurudhi(blood).
3. Tasai(muscle).
4. Kozhuppu (adipose tissue).
5. Elumbu(bone).
6. Majjai (marrow).
7. Sukkilam and Artavam (male and female hormones).

Method of Treatment:

The treatments for the imbalance of the Tridoshas are made up of the five elements. The drugs are made up of the five elements. By substituting a drug of the same constituents (guna) the equilibrium is restored. The correction of the imbalance is made by substituting the drug which is predominately of the opposite nature. An example is of *Vatham* imbalance is cold, dry thus the treatment will be oily and warmth. For inactivity of limbs, massage and activity, are prescribed. If *Pitham dosha* is increased, warmth is produced; to decrease *Pitham* , sandalwood is administered, internally or externally because of its cold characteristics.

Five type of Vayu are:

1. **Prana:** located in mouth and nostrils (inhaled); aids ingestion.
2. **Apana:** located at anal extremity (expelled); elimination, expulsion.
3. **Samana:** equalizer, aids digestion.
4. **Vyana:** circulation of blood and nutrients.
5. **Udana:** functions in upper respiratory passages

SIDDHA PHARMACY:

Mercury: Mercury occupies a very high place in Siddha medicine. It is used as a catalytic agent in many of its medicines. When mercury is used it is used in combination with sulphur. The addition of sulphur is to control the fluidity of mercury-this converts to mercuric sulphite which is insoluble in mineral acids.

Siddhas used 5 forms of mercury:

1. Mercury metal-rasam
2. Red sulphide of mercury-lingam.
3. Mercury chloride- veeram.
4. Mercury sub chloride (mercury chloride)-pooram.
5. Red oxide of mercury-rasa chenduram. Ordinary rasa chenduram (red oxide of mercury) is a poison but when it is processed as *Poorna chandrodayam* according to Siddha practice, it becomes ambrosia.

Classifications of Siddha medicine:

1. **Uppu (Lavanam):** drugs that dissolve in water and decrepitated when put into fire giving off vapours. (Water soluble inorganic compounds). There are 25 varieties and are called kara-charam, salts and alkalis.
2. **Pashanam:** drugs that do not dissolve in water but give off vapors when put into fire (water insoluble inorganic compounds).
3. **Uparasam:** drugs that do not dissolve in water (chemicals similar to Pashanam but differing in their actions) such as mica, magnetic iron, antimony, zinc sulphate, iron pyrites, ferrous sulphate.
4. **Loham:** metals and minerals alloys (water insoluble, melt in fire, solidify on cooling) such as gold, silver copper, iron, tin and lead.
5. **Rasam:** drugs which are soluble, sublime when put in fire, changing into small crystals -mercury amalgams and compounds of mercury, arsenic.
6. **Gandhakam:** sulphur insoluble in water, burns off when put into fire.
7. **Ratnas and uparatnas:** thirteen varieties are described-coral, lapis-lazli, pearls, diamonds, jade, emerald, ruby, sapphire, opal, vaikrantham, rajavantham, spatikam harin mani.

The common preparations of Siddha medicines are:

1. Bhasma (Calcined metals and minerals).
2. Churna (powders).
3. Kashaya(decoctions).
4. Lehya (confections).
5. Ghrita (ghee preparations) and Taila (oil preparations).
6. Chunna (metallic preparations which become alkaline).
7. mezhugu (waxy preparations).
8. Kattu (preparation that are impervious to water and flames

Sulphur: Calcined sulphur or red oxide of sulphur can be obtained by solidating it first by the Siddha method of purification. In small doses, it conserves the body, and it is diaphoretic and alterative. Therapeutically, it is used as both external and internal remedy against skin diseases, rheumatic arthritis, asthma, jaundice and blood poisoning.

Arsenic: As per Siddha kalpa, purified and consolidated arsenic is effective against all fevers, asthma and anaemia.

Gold: It is alterative, nervine tonic, antidote to poison and a powerful sexual stimulant. Very little is absorbed in the system. Care is taken to see that calcinations of gold is free from metallic state and lustre to ensure safe absorption in the system.

Thus, these drugs and metallic minerals can be screened for its anti-viral, immune stimulant and immuno-modulator activity. As HIV negative people have taken Kalpha drugs for rejuvenation and long life, it is believed that if Kayakapla therapy is thoroughly investigated using modern parameters it might lead one to find whether these drugs could be used in preventative or curative benefits in AIDS or other

HOMOEOPATHY SYSTEM OF MEDICINE

The word 'Homoeopathy' is derived from two Greek words, *Homois* meaning similar and *pathos* meaning suffering. Homoeopathy simply means treating diseases with remedies, prescribed in minute doses, which are capable of producing symptoms similar to the disease when taken by healthy people. It is based on the natural law of healing- "*Similia Similibus Curantur*" which means "likes are cured by likes". Dr. Samuel Hahnemann (1755-1843) gave it a scientific basis in the early 19th century. It has been serving suffering humanity for over two centuries and has withstood the upheavals of time and has emerged as a time-tested therapy.

The principle of Homoeopathy has been known since the time of *Hippocrates* from Greece, the founder of medicine, around 450 BC More than a thousand years later the Swiss alchemist *Paracelsus* employed the same system of healing based upon the principle that "like cures like". But it was not until the late 18th century that Homoeopathy as it is practiced today was evolved by the great German physician, Dr. Samuel Hahnemann. He was appalled by the medical practices of that time and set about to develop a method of healing which would be safe, gentle, and effective. He believed that human beings have a capacity for healing themselves and that the symptoms of disease reflect the individuals struggle to overcome his illness.

Hahnemann was struck by the effect that certain drugs, when taken by him while quite healthy, produced symptoms that the drug was known to cure in sick. For instance, when he took *Cinchona Bark*, which contains quinine, he became ill with symptoms that exactly mimicked intermittent fever (now called malaria). He wondered if the reason Cinchona worked against intermittent fever was because it caused symptoms indistinguishable from intermittent fever in a healthy human.

Homoeopathy is the system of treatment based on laws and principles, which are:

1. **The Law of Similars :** It is also called the Law of Cure. This law demonstrates that the selected remedy is able to produce a range of symptoms in a healthy person similar to that observed in the patient, thus leading to the principle of *Similia Similibus Curentur i.e. let likes be treated by likes*. To give a simple example the effects of peeling an onion are very similar to the symptoms of acute cold. The remedy prepared from the red onion, *Allium cepa*, is used to

treat the type of cold in which the symptoms resemble those we get from peeling onion.

2. **The Law of Single Remedy :** This law directs to choose and administer such a single remedy, which is most similar to the symptom complex of the sick person at a time.
3. **The Law of Minimum Dose :** The similar remedy selected for a sick should be prescribed in minimum dose, so that when administered there is no toxic effects on the body. It just acts as a triggering and catalytic agent to stimulate and strengthen the existing defense mechanism of the body. It does not need to be repeated frequently.

Concept of vital force: Dr. Hahnemann discovered that the human body is endowed with a force that reacts against the inimical forces, which produce disease. It becomes deranged during illness and the best-selected Homoeopathic remedies stimulate this failing vital force so that, as Hahnemann said "it can again take the reins and conduct the system on way to health".

Concept of Miasm: *Psora, Syphilis and Sycosis* are the three fundamental causes of all chronic diseases that afflict the human race as discovered by Dr. Hahnemann and called them *miasms*. This word is derived from Greek word miainein meaning 'to pollute'.

Syphilis and Sycosis are the venereal and contagious chronic diseases, whereas Psora is a non-venereal chronic disease. Psora is present from the beginning to end of life and is the root cause of most of the disease.

Principle of drug proving: To apply drugs for therapeutic use, their curative powers should be known. The proving of the drug is the method employed to know these powers and is unique to Homoeopathy as they are proved on healthy human beings. The symptoms thus known are the true record of the curative properties of a drug or the pathogenesis of a drug.

Drug dynamisation or potentisation: Drugs are prepared in such a way that they retain maximum medicinal powers without producing any toxic action on the body. It was found experimentally by Dr. Hahnemann that when diluted drugs are powerfully successes they develop lasting medicinal powers.

PREPARATION AND STANDARDIZATION OF AYURVEDIC FORMULATIONS

AYURVEDIC FORMULATIONS

Ayurvedic formulations are:

1. Arista and Asavas
2. Gutikas
3. Tailas
4. Churnas.
5. Lehyas.
6. Bhasmas

ARISTA AND ASAVAS

Asavas and Aristas are medicinal preparation made by soaking the drugs either in powder form or in the form of decoction (Kasaya), in a solution of sugar or jaggery, for a specified period of time. During this process fermentation takes place and alcohol is generated which facilitates the extraction of active principles contained in the drugs. The alcohol so generated also serves as a preservative.

Method of preparation:

1. **Preparation of Aristas:** The drug is coarsely powdered and Kasaya is prepared. The Kasaya is strained and kept in fermentation vessel. Sugar,

jaggery or honey, as required, is dissolved, boiled and added. The mouth of the vessel is covered with an earthen lid and the edges sealed with clay-smeared cloth wound in seven consecutive layers. A constant temperature is maintained for fermentation by keeping the container either in a special room, in an underground cellar or in a heap of paddy. After a specified period the lid is removed and the contents examined to ascertain whether fermentation has been completed. The fluid is first decanted and then strained after two or three days. When the fine suspended particles settle down, it is strained and bottled.

2. **Preparation of Asavas:** The Jaggery or sugar is dissolved in the required quantity of water, boiled and cooled. This is poured into the fermentation vessel. Fine powder of the drugs is added in the container which is covered with a lid and the edges are sealed with clay smeared cloth wound in seven consecutive layers. A constant temperature is maintained for fermentation by keeping the container either in a special room, in an underground cellar or in a heap of paddy. After a specified period the lid is removed and the contents examined to ascertain whether fermentation has been completed. The fluid is first decanted and then strained after two or three days. When the fine suspended particles settle down, it is strained and bottled.

Precaution:

1. The filtered Asavas or Aristas should be clear without froth at the top.
2. It should not become sour.
3. The preparation has the characteristic aromatic alcoholic odour.

Storage: They should be stored in well-stoppered bottles or jars.

Marketed preparation:

1. Asavas

a. Arvindasava.
b. Kumaryasava.
c. Vasakasava.

2. Aristas:
   a. Abhyarista.
   b. Balarista.
   c. Dasmularista.
   d. Vidangarista.

GUTIKAS

These are solid dosage form of medicament meant for oral administration prepared by hand or machine.

Method of preparation:

The material are mixed together and a suitable liquid is incorporated to make the mass wet. This wet mass is kneaded in between the fingers so as to get a uniform mass. The mass so prepared is rolled on a hard surface so as to make a pencil which is then divided into desired number of pieces and each piece is rounded by finger.

Precautions:

1. The material should be finely powdered.
2. Diluents may be added when the quantity of drugs is small. Lactose is used as a diluents, when drug is potent.
3. Size should be within limits.
4. Only soluble substance are used which can be dissolve in stomach.
5. If pill breaks then a binding agent like gum acacia may be added.
6. It should not be too soft or too hard.

Preservation: It should be store in air tight container.

Marketed preparations:

1. Lasunadi Gutika.
2. Marma Gutica.
3. Mritsanjiani Gutika.

TAILAS

Tailas are the liquid or semisolid dosage form of medicament which is meant for internal and external use.

Tailas are preparations in which tail (oil) is boiled with prescribed Kasaya (decoction) and kalkas of the drug according to the formula. This process ensures absorption of the active therapeutic principles of the ingredients.

Methods of preparation: It involves three essential components for the preparation of Tailas:

1. Liquid (water)
2. Fine paste of the drug
3. Taila (sneha dravya)

The fine paste of the drug and the liquid are mixed together and ghee is then added, boiled and stirred well continuously so that the paste is not allowed to adhere to vessel walls. When all the liquid contents have evaporated, the moisture content in the fine paste of the drug will also begin to evaporate. At this stage it has to be stirred more often and carefully to ensure that the fine paste of the drug does not stick to the bottom of the vessel. The fine paste is taken out with the help of ladle and tested from time to time to know the condition and stage of the pakam. When the pakam is harder when put in fire burns without any crackling noise indicates the optimal stage for oral intake. In the beginning the boiling should be on mild fire and in the end also it should be mild fire. In the

Characteristics: They will have colour, odour and taste of the drugs used and have the consistency of the oil. When considerable quantity of milk is used in the preparation, the oil become thick due to ghrita and in cold season may condense further.

Preservation: They are preserve in glass, polythene or aluminium container.

Marketed preparation:

1. Pinda Taila.
2. Bhringaraja Taila.
3. Narayana Taila.

CHURAN

These are solid dosage form of medicament meant for internal use.

These are two types:

1. **Simple churan:** It contains only one medicament.
2. **Compound churan:** It contains two or more than two medicaments.

Method of preparation: The drugs are cleaned and dried properly. They are finely powdered and sieved. If more than one drug are present then each one is separately powdered, sieved, accurately weighed and then all mixed together. The powder is fine to the extent of at least 80 mesh sieves. It should not adhere together or become moist. The finer powder has better therapeutic value.

Preservation: It should be stored in the air tight containers.

Precaution:

1. Thoroughly cleaned and dried drugs should be used for the preparation of churans.
2. They should be finely sifted.
3. Each substance should be powdered separately and then mixed.
4. Pestle and mortar used for reducing the particle size and mixing the substances should be clean and dry.
5. They must be stored in a dry container.
6. They should not be prepared in rainy season.
7. They should dissolve in the stomach contents.

The dose is 2-3 gm which may be increased or decreased according to age and severity of disease. It is administered with water, milk, fruit juices or any other suitable liquid depending on the nature of disease. It may be given by mixing with gur or honey in equal quantity, with sugar twice the quantity and with milk four times the quantities as that of drug.

Marketed preparation:

1. Triphala churna.
2. Sudarshan churna.
3. Drakshadi Churna.

AVALEHA

Avaleha is a semisolid preparation of the drugs prepared with the addition of jaggery or sugar candy and boiled with prescribed drug juice or decoction.

Method of preparation: These preparations generally have:

1. Kasayam or other liquid.
2. Jaggery or sugar-candy.
3. Powder or pulps of certain drugs

4. Gee or oil
5. Honey.

Jaggery, sugar or sugar candy is dissolved in the liquid and stained to remove the foreign particles. This solution is boiled over a moderate fire. When the paka (phanita) is thready, when pressed between two fingers or when it sinks in water without getting easily dissolved, it should be removed from the fire. Fine powder of drugs are then added in small quantities and stirred continuously and vigorously to form a homogenous mixture. Gee or oil, if required, is added while the preparation is still hot and mixed well. Honey is added when the preparation is cool and mixed well.

The Aveleha should neither be hard nor be a thick fluid. When pulp of the drug is added and gee or oil is present, this can be rolled between fingers. Growth of the fungus indicates deterioration. The colour and smell of the preparation depend on the drugs used.

Preservation: It should be kept in glass or porcelain jars.

Marketed Formulation:

1. Suranavaleha.
2. Draksavaleha.
3. Chyawanprash

BHASMA

Bhasma (Calcinated residue) is solid dosage form of medicament meant for internal use. Generally pearls, iron, gold, silver, lead, tin, zinc, black mica etc are used for their preparation. Bhasma means an ash obtained through incineration. Bhasma is the powder of a substance obtained by calcinations. It is applied to the metals and mineral products which are prepared by special processes in closed crucibles in pits and with cow dung cakes (puta).

Method of preparation:

Two steps:

1. **Sodhana**: Bhasma are prepared from minerals, metals, marine and animal products. In Ayurveda, the process of purification is called Sodhana, which is of two types:
   (i) **Samanya Sodhana:** It is applicable to a large number of metals or minerals, as heating the thin sheets of the metals and immersing them in Taila, takra, gomutra, etc.
   (ii) **Viesa Sodhana:** It is applicable only to certain drugs and in certain preparations.

2. Murana: The purified drug is put into a khalva (stone mortar and pestle) and ground with juices of the specified plants or Kasaya of the drugs mentioned for particular mineral or metal. It is ground specified period of time. Then small cakes (cakrikas) are made. These cakes are dried well under sunlight and placed in one single layer in a shallow earthen plate (sarava) and closed with another plate. The edge is sealed with clay smeared cloth in seven consecutive layers and dried. A pit is dug in an open space. Half of the pit is filled with cow dung cakes. The sealed earthen container is placed in it and the remaining space is filled with more cow dug cakes. Fire is put in all four sides and the middle of the pit. When the burning is over, it is allowed to cool completely. The earthen container is removed; the seal is open and content taken out. The medicine is ground into a fine powder in a khalva. This process of triturating with the juice, making cakrikas and giving puts, is repeated as many times as prescribed.

Storage: They are preserved in air tight glass or earthen container.

Marketed Formulation:

1. Lauha Bhasma.
2. Shankha Bhasma.

3. Surarna Bhasma.
4. Tamra Bhasma.

STANDARDIZATION OF AYURVEDIC FORMULATIONS

1. Monograph: Title: - Sanskrit name.
2. Description: Macroscopical characters or gross external morphology.
3. Identification tests.
4. Tests for detection of adulterants.
5. Loss of drying.
6. Foreign matter.
7. Solubility.
8. Fat content: Taila and Ghrita.
9. Acid value/Saponification value/ Iodine value: Taila and Ghrita.
10. Resin: Guggulu.
11. Ash values:
    a. Total ash
    b. Acid insoluble ash.
12. Extractive values:
    a. Water soluble extractive value
    b. Alcohol soluble extractive value.
13. Total solid.
14. Volatile matter.
15. Sugar
    a. Total sugar.
    b. Reducing sugar.
    c. Non-reducing sugar.
16. pH.

17.Alcohol content: Asava and arishta.

18.Assay for:

a. Aluminium/ arsenic/ borate/ Calcium.
b. Camphor/ Chloride/ Copper/ Gold/ Iron.
c. Lead/ Magnesium/ Mercury/ Phosphate.
d. Potassium/ Silica/ Siler/ Sodium.
e. Sulpher/ Sulphate/ Tin.
f. Total alkaloids

19.Dissentrigation test: For pills and tablet.

20.Weight Uniformity: For pills and tablet.

21.Therapeutic indications.

22.Dose.

MACROSCOPICAL CHARACTERS

Macroscopic identity of medicinal plant materials is based on shape, size, colour, surface characteristics, texture, fracture characteristic and appearance of the cut surface.

1. **Size:** A graduated ruler in millimeters is adequate for the measurement of the length, width and thickness of crude materials. Small seeds and fruits may be measured by aligning 10 of them on a sheet of calibrated paper, with 1 mm spacing between lines, and dividing the result by 10.
2. **Colour:** Examine the untreated sample under diffuse daylight may be used. The colour of the sample should be compared with that of a reference sample.
3. **Surface charactestics, texture and fracture characteristics:** Examine the untreated sample. If necessary, a magnifying lens may be used. Wetting with water or reagents, as required, may be necessary to observe the characteristics of a cut surface. Touch the material to determine if it is soft or hard; bend and

rupture it to obtain information on brittleness and the appearance of the fracture plane- whether it is fibrous, smooth, rough and granular, etc.

4. **Odour**: If the material is expected to be innocuous, place a small portion of the sample in the palm of the hand or a beaker of suitable size, and slowly and repeatedly inhale the air over the material. If no distinct odour is perceptible, crush the sample between the thumb and index finger or between the palms of the hands using gentle pressure. If the material is known to be dangerous, crush by mechanical means and then pour a small quantity of boiling water onto the crushed sample in a beaker. First, determine the strength of the odour (none, weak, distinct, strong) and then the odour sensation (aromatic, fruity, musty, moldy, rancid, etc.). A direct comparison of the odour with a defined substance is advisable (e.g. peppermint should have an odour similar to menthol, clove a similar to eugenol).
5. **Taste:**

   Chirata : Bitter

   Glycyrrhiza : Sweet

   Lemon : Sour.

DETERMINATION OF WATER AND VOLATILE MATTER

An excess of water in medicinal plant materials will encourage microbial growth, the presence of fungi or insect, and deterioration following hydrolysis. Limits for water content should therefore be set for every given plant material. This is especially important for materials that absorb moisture easily or deteriorate quickly in the presence of water. Following methods are use as:

1. **Azeotropic method:** The Azeotropic gives a direct measurement of the water present in the material being examined. When the sample is distilled together with an immiscible solvent, such as toluene R or Xylene R, the water present in

the sample is absorbed by the solvent. The water and the solvent are distilled together and separated in the receiving tube on cooling. If the solvent is anhydrous, water may remain absorbed in it leading to false results. It is therefore advisable to saturate the solvent with water before use.

2. **Loss of drying:** Drying can be carried out either by heating to 100- 105^{0}C or in a desiccator over phosphorus pentoxide R under atmospheric or reduced pressure at room temperature for a specified period of time. The desiccation method is especially useful for materials that melt to a sticky mass at elevated temperature.

LOSS OF DRYING

Weigh a glass- stopper, shallow weighing bottle that has been dried under same condition to be employed in the determination. Transfer to the bottle the quantity of the sample, cover it and accurately weigh the bottle and the contents. Distribute the sample as evenly as practicable by gentle side wise shaking to a depth not exceeding 10 mm. Place the loaded bottle in the drying chamber (oven or desiccator), remove the stopper the stopper and leave it also in the chamber. Dry the sample to constant weight or for the specified time and at the temperature. After drying is completed, open the drying chamber, close the bottle promptly and allow it to cool to room temperature in a desiccator before weighing. Weigh the bottle and the contents.

FOREIGN MATTER

Foreign matter is material consisting of any or all of the following:

1. Parts of medicinal plant material or material other than those named with the limits specified for the plant material concerned.

2. Any organism, part or product of an organism, other than that named in the specification and description of the plant material concerned.
3. Mineral admixtures not adhering to the medicinal plant materials such as soil, stones, sand, and dust
4. Moulds, insect or other animal contamination.

Method: Weigh accurately 100gm to 500 gm of original sample and spread it out in a thin layer. Inspect the sample with the unaided eye or with the use of a 6X lens and separate the foreign organic matter manually as completely as possible. Weigh and determine the percentage of foreign organic matter from the weight of the drug taken. Use the maximum quantity of sample for coarse or bulky drugs.

ASH VALUES

Ash values are helpful in determining the quality and purity of crude drugs, especially in powder form. The objective of ashing vegetable drugs is to remove all traces of organic matter, which may otherwise interfere in an analytical determination. On incineration, crude drugs normally leave an ash usually consisting of carbonates, phosphates and silicates of sodium, potassium, calcium and magnesium.

Determination of Ash values:

1. **Total ash:** Take about 2 or 3 g, accurately weighed, of the ground drug in a tared platinum or silica dish previously ignited and weighed. Scatter the ground drug in a fine even layer on the bottom of the dish. Incerated by gradually increasing the heat- not exceeding dull red heat- until free from carbon, cool and weigh. If a carbon free ash can not be obtained in this way, exhaust the charred mass with hot water, collect the residue on an ashless filter paper, incerate the residue and filter paper, add the filtrate, evaporate to dryness and

ignite at low temperature. Calculate the percentage of ash with reference to the air dried drug.

2. **Acid- insoluble ash:** Boil the total ash with for five minutes with 25 ml of dilute hydrochloric acid, collect the insoluble matter in a Gooch crucible or on an ashless filter paper, wash with hot water, ignite, and weigh. Calculate the percentage of acid- insoluble ash with reference to the air dried drug.
3. **Water- soluble ash:** Boil the total ash for 5 minutes with 25 ml of water; collect the insoluble matter in a Gooch crucible or on an ashless filter paper, wash with hot water, and ignite to constant weight at a low temperature. Subtract the weight of insoluble matter from the weight of the ash; the difference in weight represents the water- soluble ash. Calculate the percentage of water- soluble ash with reference to the air dried drug.
4. **Sulphated ash:** A silica crucible was heated to redness for 10 minutes, allowed to cool in desiccator and weighed. 1 g of substance was accurately weighed and transferred to the crucible. It was ignited gently at first, until the substance was thoroughly charred. Then the residue was cooled and moistened with 1 ml concentrated sulfuric acid, heated gently until white fumes are no longer evolved and ignited at 800° ± 25°C until all black particles have disappeared. The ignition was conducted in a place protected from air currents. The crucible was allowed to cool, and a few drops of concentrated sulfuric acid were added and heated. Ignited as before, allowed to cool, and weighed. The operation was repeated until two successive weighing does not differ by more than 0.5 mg. Calculate the percentage of Sulphated ash with reference to the air dried drug.

EXTRACTIVE VALUES

Extractive values of crude drugs are useful for their evaluation, especially when the constituents of a drug can not be readily estimated by any other means. Further, these values indicate the nature of the constituents present in a crude drug.

Determination of extractive values:

1. Alcohol- soluble extractive: Macerate 5 g of the air- dried drug, coarsely powdered, with 100 ml of alcohol of the specified strength in a closed flask for 24 hrs shaking frequently during 6 hrs and allowing to stand for 18 hrs. Filter rapidly taking precautions against loss of alcohol; evaporate 25 percentage of alcohol-soluble extractive with reference to the air- dried drug.

2. Water –soluble extractive:

Method-I: Macerate 5 g of the air- dried drug, coarsely powdered, with 100 ml of chloroform water of the specified strength in a closed flask for 24 hrs shaking frequently during 6 hrs and allowing to stand for 18 hrs. Filter rapidly taking precautions against loss of alcohol; evaporate 25 percentage of alcohol- soluble extractive with reference to the air- dried drug.

Method-II: Add 5 g to 50 ml f water at 80^{0}C in a stoppered flask. Shake well and allow standing for 10 minutes; cooling to 15^{0}C and adding 2 g kiesslguhr; filtering. Transfer 5 ml of filtrate to a tared evaporating basin 7.5 cm in diameter, evaporate the solvent on a water- bath, continue drying for half an hour, finally dry in a steam oven for 2 hrs and weigh the residue. Calculate the percentage of water soluble extractive with reference to the air- dried drug.

ACID VALUE

The acid value is the number of mg of potassium hydroxide required to neutralize the free acid in 1 g of the substance.

Determination of acid value:

Weigh accurately about 10 g of the substance into a 250 ml flask, and add 50 ml of a mixture of equal volume of alcohol and solvent ether, which has been neutralized after addition of 1ml of solution of phenolphthalein. Heat gently on a water bath, if necessary, until the substance has completely melted, titrate with 0.1

N potassium hydroxide, shaking constantly until a pink colour which persist for 15 seconds is obtained. Note the number of ml required. Calculate the acid value from the following formula:

$$\text{Acid value} = \frac{a \times 0.00561 \times 1000}{w}$$

a = Number of ml of 0.1 N potassium hydroxide required

w = Weight in g of the substance taken.

SAPONIFICATION VALUE

The Saponification value is the number of mg of potassium hydroxide required to neutralize the fatty acid, resulting from the complete hydrolysis of 1 g of the oil or fat.

Determination of Saponification value:

Weigh accurately about 2 g of the substance in a tared 250 ml flask, add 25 ml of the alcoholic solution of potassium hydroxide, attach a reflex condenser, and boil on a water bath for one hour frequently rotating the contents of the flask; cool and add 1 ml of solution of phenolphthalein and titrate the excess of alkali with 0.5 N hydrochloric acid. Calculate the Saponification value from the following formula:

$$\text{Saponification value} = \frac{(b-a) \times 0.02805 \times 1000}{w}$$

w = Weight in g of the substance taken

IODINE VALUE

The iodine value is the number which expresses in grams the quantity of Iodine, which is absorbed by 100 g of the substance.

Determination of Iodine value:

Iodine Monochloride Method: Place the substance, accurately weighed, in a dry iodine flask; add 10 ml of carbon trichloride, and dissolve. Add 20 ml of Iodine Monochloride solution insert the stopper previously moistened with solution of potassium iodide and allow to stand in a dark place at a temperature of about 17^0 for 30 minutes. Add 15 ml of solution of potassium iodide and 100 ml of water; shake, and titrate with 0.1 N sodium thiosulphate, using solution of starch as indicator. Note the number of ml required (a). At the same time carry out the operation in exactly, the same manner, but without the substance being tested, and note the number of ml of 0.1 N sodium thiosulphate required (b).

$$\text{Iodine value} = \frac{(b - a) \times 0.01269 \times 100}{w}$$

w = Weight in gm of the substance taken

Determination of pesticide residues

1. Determination of Chlorides:

a. **Apparatus:** The determination is made with a spectrophotometer capable of measuring absorbance at 460 nm using absorption cells with path-lengths of 2 cm and 10 cm

b. **Procedure:** Place 15 ml of the solution obtained after combustion in a 50 ml conical flask together with 1ml of ferric ammonium sulphate (0.25 mol/l) and 3 ml of mercuric thiocyanate. Swirl the contents of the flask and allow to stand for 10 minutes. Transfer a portion of the solution to a 2 cm cell and measure the absorbance at 460 nm using water in the reference cell. The reading should be made promptly to minimize absorption of chloride from the air.

   i. Prepare a standard solution of sodium chloride containing 5 μg of chloride per ml. transfer aliquots of this solution (0 ml, 2ml, 4 ml, 6 ml, 8 ml and 10 ml) into a series of 50 ml conical flasks and dilute to 15 ml with water. Develop the colour and measure the absorbance as describe above. Plot the absorbance against the chloride content of the dilutions in µg per ml and interpolate the chloride content of the solutions of the material tested.

2. **Limit test for Arsenic:**
    a. **Apparatus:** The apparatus consists of a 100 ml bottle or conical flask closed with a rubber or ground- glass stopper through which passes a glass tube. The lower part of the tube is drawn to an internal diameter of 1.0 mm, and 15 mm from its tip is a lateral orifice 2 to 3 mm in diameter. When the tube is in position in the stopper the lateral orifice should be at least 3 mm below the lower surface of the stopper. The upper end of the tube has a perfectly flat surface at right angles to the axis of the tube. A second glass tube of the same internal diameter and 30 mm long, with a similar flat surface, is placed in contact springs or clips. Into the lower tube insert 50 to 60 mg of lead acetate cotton, loosely packed or a small plug of cotton and a rolled piece of lead acetate paper weighing 50 to 60 mg. between the flat surfaces of the tubes place a disc or Small Square of mercuric chloride paper large enough to cover the orifice of the tube.
    b. **Procedure:** the test solution is introducing into the bottle or conical flask; add 5 ml of 1 M potassium iodide and 10 g of Zinc AsT. Immediately assemble the apparatus and immerse the flask in a water- bath at a temperature such that a uniform evolution of gas is maintained. After 40 minutes any stain produced on the mercuric chloride paper is not more intense than that obtained by treating in the same manner 1.0 ml of arsenic standard solution (10 ppm As) diluted to 50 ml with water.

3. **Determination of Heavy Metals:**

   a. **Standard solution:** Into a 50 ml Nessler cylinder pipette 1.0 ml of lead standard solution (20 ppm Pb) and dilute with water to 25 ml. adjust with dilute acetic acid or dilute ammonia solution to a pH between 3.0 and 4.0, dilute with water to about 35 ml and mix.

   b. **Test solution:** Into a 50 ml Nessler cylinder place 25 ml of the solution prepared for the test as directed in the individual monograph or dissolve the specified quantity of the substance being examined in sufficient water to produce 25 ml. adjust with dilute acetic acid or dilute ammonia solution to a pH between 3 to 4 dilute with water to about 35 ml and mix.

   c. **Procedure:** To each of the cylinders containing the standard solution and test solution respectively add 10 ml of freshly prepared hydrogen sulphide solution, mix, dilute to 50 ml with water, allow to stand for 5 minutes and view downwards over a white surface; the colour produced with the test solution is not more intense than that produced with the standard solution.

DISINTEGRATION TEST

Disintegration test is very important and necessary for all the tablets and pills to be swallowed because the dissolution rate depends upon the time of disintegration which ultimately affects the rate of absorption of drugs.

Disintegration test apparatus consists of a glass or plastic tube which is open at one end and the other end is fitted with a rust proof No.-10 mesh sieve. The tube is suspended in a bath of water or suitable liquid which is thermostatically maintained at a temperature of 37^{0}C. the tube is allowed to move up and down at a constant rate i.e. 30 times per minute through distance of 75 mm. the volume of the liquid and distance of movement is adjusted in such a way that at the highest point the mesh screen just breaks the surface of the liquid to give a turbulent movement to the tablets and at the lowest point the mesh screen remains about 2.5 cm above the bottom of the container.

About 5 tablets are placed in the tube along with a plastic disk over the tablets unless otherwise stated in the monograph. The plastic disk does not allow the tablets to float and imparts a slight pressure on the tablets. The tube is allowed to move up and down and disintegration time noted when all the tablets have passed through the sieve

IDENTIFICATION TEST

1. Test for alkaloids

S.No.	Reagent	Observation
1	Mayer's Reagent (Potassium mercuric iodide solution)	Creamy precipitate
2	Wagner's reagent (Aqueous iodine solution)	Reddish brown precipitate
3	Tannic acid test (Freshly prepared tannic acid)	Precipitate which is soluble in dilute acid or ammonia solution
4	Dragendorff's reagent (Potassium bismuth iodide solution)	Reddish brown precipitate
5	Hager's reagents (Saturated picric acid solution)	Yellow precipitate

2. Test for glycosides:

a. Tests for saponin glycosides:

i. **Foam test:** Shake the drug extract or dry powder vigorously with water. Persistent foam observed.

ii. **Haemolytic test:** Add drug extract or dry powder to one drop of blood placed on glass slide. Haemolytic zone appears.

b. Test for anthraquinone glycoside:

i. **Borntranger's Test**: Powdered leaves of Senna are boiled with dilute sulphuric acid, Filtered and cooled. The filtrate is extracted with chloroform or benzene and dilute ammonia is added to it. The ammonical layer becomes pink to red due to the presence of anthraquinones derivative.

ii. **Modified Anthraquinones Test:** Take 0.1 gm of drug and add 5ml of 5% solution of ferric chloride and 5ml dilute hydrochloric acid and heat on boiling water-bath for 5 minutes, cool the solution and shake gently with a organic solvent like benzene. Separate the organic solvent layer and add an equal volume of dilute ammonia. A pinkish red color is formed in ammonical layer. This test is of C. glycoside.

c. **Chemical tests for cardiac glycosides:**

i. **Raymond's test:** To the drug, add a few ml of 50% ethanol and 0.1 ml of 1 % solution of m- dinitrobenzene in ethanol. To this solution, add 2-3 drops of 20% sodium hydroxide solution. Violet colors appears, this is due to presence of active methylene group.

ii. **Legal test:** To the drug, add few ml of pyridine and 2drops of nitroprusside and a drop of 20% sodium hydroxide solution. A deep red color is produced.

iii. **Killer killiani test:** Glycoside is dissolved in a mixture of 1 % ferric sulphate solution in (5%) glacial acetic acid. Add one or two drop of concentrated sulphuric acid. A blue color develops due to the presence of deoxy sugar.

iv. **Xanthydrol test:** The crude is heated with 0.1 to 5% solution of Xanthydrol in glacial acetic acid containing 1% hydrochloric acid. A red colour is produced due to the presence of 2-deoxysugar.

v. Baljet test: Take a piece of lamina or thick section of the leaf and add sodium picrate reagent. If glycoside is present yellow to orange colour will be seen.

vi. **Kedde test:** A solution of glycosides is treated with a small amount of Kedde reagent (Mix equal volumes of a 2% solution of 3, 5 dinitrobenzoic acid in menthol and a 7.5% aqueous solution of KOH). Development of a blue or violet colour that faded out in 1to 2 hrs shows it presence of cardinoloids.

d. Cyanogenetic glycoside

i. **Ferriferrocyanide test:** Macerate 1 g of the powdered drug with 5 ml of alcoholic KOH for 5 min. transfer it to an aqueous solution containing $FeSO_4$ and $FeCl_3$, and maintain at 60-70^{0}C for 10 minutes. Now transfer the contents to HCl (20%) when the appearance of a distinct Prussian blue colour confirms the presence of HCN.

ii. **Precipitation of Hg from $HgNO_3$**: The reduction of aqueous mercurous nitrite solution to metallic Hg by HCN being observed by an instant formation of black metallic Hg in the cells.

iii. **Cuprocyanate Test:** To saturate the pieces of filter paper in a freshly prepared solution of guaic resin dissolved in absolute ethanol and allows them to dry completely in air. Now, carefully moisten a piece of the above paper with a very dilute solution of $CuSO_4$ and place it into contact with a freshly exposed surface of the drug. In case, HCN is generated, it will give rise to a distinct strain on the paper.

e. Flavonoid glycosides:

i. **Shinoda test**: to dry powder or extract, add 5 ml of 95% ethanol, few drops of conc. HCl and 0.5 g magnesium turnings. Pink colour observed.

ii. To small quantity of residue, add lead acetate solution. Yellow coloured precipitate is formed.

iii. Addition of increasing amount of sodium hydroxide to the residue show yellow colouration, which decolouration after addition of acid.

f. Saponin glycoside:

i. **Foam test:** Shake the drug extract or dry powder vigorously with water. Persistent foam observed.

ii. **Haemolytic test:** Add drug extract or dry powder to one drop of blood placed on glass slide. Haemolytic zone appears.

3. Tests for tannins:

a. **Gelatin test:** To a solution of tannin, aqueous solution of gelatin and sodium chloride are added. A white buff coloured precipitate is formed.

b. **Goldbeater's skin test:** A small piece of goldbeater skin (membrane prepared from the intestine of an ox) is soaked in 20% hydrochloric acid, ringed with distilled water and placed in a solution of tannin for 5 minutes. The skin piece is washed with distilled water and kept in a solution of ferrous sulphate. A brown or black colour is produced on the skin due presence of tannins.

c. **Phenazone test:** A mixture of aqueous extract of a drug and sodium acid phosphate is heated and cooled and filtered. A solution of phenazone is added to the filtrate. A bulky coloured precipitate is formed.

d. **Match stick test (Catechin test):** a match stick is dipped in aqueous plant extract, dried near burner and moistened with concentrated hydrochloric acid. On warming near flame, the matchstick wood turns pink or red due to formation of phloroglucinol.

e. **Chlorogenic acid test**: An extract of chlorogenic acid containing drug is treated with aqueous ammonia. A green colour is formed on exposure to air.

f. **Vanillin-hydrochloric acid test:** Sample solution and added vanillin-hydrochloric acid reagent (Vanillin 1 gm, alcohol 10 ml, concentrated hydrochloric acid 10 ml). A pink or red colour is formed due to formation of phloroglucinol.

4. Test for carbohydrate:

a. **Molish test**: To 5 ml of sample solution in a test tube, add 2 drops of molish's reagent (5% solution of α -naphthol in alcohol). Mix thoroughly. Incline the tube and allow about 3 ml of concentrated H_2SO_4 to flow down the side tube, thus forming a layer of acid beneath the sugar. A reddish violet zone appears at the junction between the two liquids.

b. **Fehling Test:** Take Fehling solution (A + B) in test tube, add sample solution and boil. Formation of a precipitate of brownish-red cuprous oxide, presence of reducing sugar.

c. **Benedict test:** Take sample solution and add benedict reagent, mix well, boil the mixture vigorously for two minutes. To produce red, yellow or green colour precipitate, presence of reducing sugar.

d. **Iodine test:** Sample solution and add iodine solution to produce blue colour presence of polysaccharides.

e. **Barfoed's test:** sample solution and add Barfoed's reagent [copper acetate (13.3 gm) and glacial acetic acid (1.8ml)], boil for 3 minutes and cool. Red colour produced. Presence of monosaccharide.

f. **Seliwanoff's test:** Sample solution and add seliwanoff's reagent [resorcinol (50 mg) in conc. HCl (33 ml, 33%)], boil for 2 minutes. Red colour is produced. Presence of fructose.

5. **Test for lipid:**
   a. **Salkowski test:** Sample dissolve in chloroform and add equal volume of concentrated H_2SO_4. To produce bluish-red to cherry to cherry-red colour.
   b. **Liebermann- Burchard test:** Sample is dissolve in chloroform in a dry test tube. Add few drop of acetic anhydride and few drop of concentrated H_2SO_4. The solution becomes red, then blue and finally bluish- green in colour.
6. **Test for proteins:**
   a. **Biuret test:** To 2-3 ml of sample solution in a test tube and add equal volume of 10% solution of NaOH, mix thoroughly, and add 0.5% solution of copper sulphate drop by drop mixing between drop, until a purplish-violet or pinkish violet colour is produced.
7. **Tests for amino acid:**
   a. **Ninhydrin test:** Take 3 ml of sample solution and add 0.5 ml of Ninhydrin solution (0.1%), boil for one minute. Produce blue colour. Presence of amino acid.
   b. **Millon's test:** Take 3 ml of sample solution and add 2 ml of Millon's reagent (1 part of mercury dissolved in 2 part of conc. nitric acid) and boil. White ppt turn red on heating. Tyrosine is present.
   c. **Sakaguchi Reaction:** Take 3 ml of sample solution and add 2 drops of α-naphthol (1%) and add 1 ml NaOH solution and add 2 ml drop of sodium hypobromide. Bright red colour is produced. Argenine is present. Take 3 ml of sample solution and add 5 drops of lead acetate and add sodium

hydroxide solution (40%) drop by drop until the ppt dissolves and boil. Brown or black colour ppt is produced. Presence of cystine and cysteine.

MCQs (Objective):

1. What does the term "Ayurveda" mean?
   a) Ancient Medicine
   b) Science of Herbs
   c) Science of Life
   d) Study of Ancient Texts
2. Which Ayurvedic discipline deals with Pediatrics?
   a) Kaya Chikitsa
   b) Kaumar Bhritya
   c) Bhoot Vidya
   d) Shalakya
3. In Ayurveda, how many Panchamahabhutas or basic elements are there?
   a) Three
   b) Four
   c) Five
   d) Six
4. Who is credited with evolving Homoeopathy as it is practiced today?
   a) Hippocrates
   b) Paracelsus
   c) Dr. Samuel Hahnemann
   d) Agasthya
5. According to the Siddha system, which element is NOT one of the five basic elements?
   a) Munn

b) Neer

c) Aakasam

d) Wood

6. In the Unani system of medicine, how many essentials are there?

   a) Four

   b) Five

   c) Six

   d) Seven

7. Which Ayurvedic formulation involves fermentation and the generation of alcohol?

   a) Gutikas

   b) Tailas

   c) Arista and Asavas

   d) Churnas

8. Which among the following is NOT a principle of Homoeopathy?

   a) Law of Similars

   b) Law of Minimum Dose

   c) Law of Maximum Potency

   d) Law of Single Remedy

9. Which substance is considered to have a high place in Siddha medicine and is used as a catalytic agent?

   a) Gold

   b) Sulphur

   c) Mercury

   d) Arsenic

10. Which system of medicine believes in the natural law of healing- "Similia Similibus Curantur"?

a) Siddha

b) Ayurveda

c) Unani

d) Homoeopathy

11. Bhasma is obtained from:

a) Incineration.

b) Evaporation.

c) Distillation.

d) Crystallization.

12. The Sodhana process related to Ayurveda is for:

a) Purification.

b) Filtration.

c) Preservation.

d) Oxidation.

13. Which of the following is a marketed formulation of Bhasma?

a) Lauha Bhasma.

b) Kajal.

c) Chyawanprash.

d) Triphala.

14. The determination of water content in medicinal plant materials is crucial because:

a) It gives color.

b) It increases weight.

c) It encourages microbial growth.

d) It adds flavor.

15. Which test determines the presence of saponin glycosides by observing persistent foam?

a) Hager's test.

b) Kedde test.

c) Foam test.

d) Legal test.

16. What does the Iodine value represent?

a) Quantity of Iodine absorbed by 10 g of the substance.

b) Quantity of Iodine absorbed by 100 g of the substance.

c) Quantity of Iodine released by 100 g of the substance.

d) Quantity of Iodine neutralized by 1 g of the substance.

17. The acid value of a substance denotes the number of mg of potassium hydroxide required to: a) Evaporate the free acid.

b) Precipitate the free acid.

c) Neutralize the free acid.

d) Convert the free acid.

18. A test where the drug extract or dry powder is shaken vigorously with water to observe persistent foam is called:

a) Kedde test.

b) Foam test.

c) Wagner's reagent test.

d) Benedict test.

19. Which of the following tests is used to determine the presence of carbohydrates that produce a blue color?

a) Liebermann- Burchard test.

b) Ninhydrin test.

c) Iodine test.

d) Salkowski test.

20. Total ash value in a drug helps in determining:

a) Flavor.

b) Color.

c) Purity.

d) Solubility.

Short Answer Type Questions (Subjective):

1. Briefly describe the concept of "Miasm" in Ayurveda.
2. Explain the significance of mercury in Siddha medicine.
3. How is the Law of Similars applied in Homoeopathy?
4. Describe the process of preparing Aristas in Ayurveda.
5. What are the roles that Rasayana therapy plays in Ayurveda?
6. Discuss the significance of the Tridoshas in Siddha medicine.
7. How is the diagnosis done in Ayurveda?
8. What are the primary differences between Asavas and Aristas?
9. Describe the concept of "vital force" in Homoeopathy.
10. Explain the significance of the five Panchamahabhutas in Ayurveda.
11. What is the significance of Bhasma in Ayurvedic medicine?
12. Describe the two types of Sodhana.
13. Explain the process of Murana in preparing Bhasma.
14. Why are ash values important in determining the quality of crude drugs?
15. How is the saponification value determined?
16. Describe the Biuret test for proteins.
17. What are the potential implications of excess water in medicinal plant materials?
18. How is the acid value of a substance determined?
19. What is the significance of the disintegration test for tablets and pills?
20. Describe the Wagner's reagent test for alkaloids.

Long Answer Type Questions (Subjective):

1. Discuss in detail the principles and concepts underlying the Ayurvedic system of medicine and its approach to the treatment of diseases.
2. Describe the origin, principles, and concepts of the Siddha system of medicine, highlighting the significance of metals and minerals in its therapeutics.
3. Compare and contrast the Ayurvedic, Unani, Siddha, and Homoeopathy systems of medicine in terms of their principles, diagnosis, and treatment methodologies.
4. Elaborate on the preparation, precautions, and preservation of Gutikas in Ayurveda.
5. Discuss the role and significance of mercury, gold, and sulphur in Siddha pharmacy, explaining their therapeutic applications.
6. Discuss in detail the method of preparation of Bhasma and its significance in Ayurvedic medicine.
7. Describe the various tests for determining the presence of glycosides in a sample. How do these tests aid in identifying specific types of glycosides?
8. Explain the importance of standardization of Ayurvedic formulations. Highlight the various tests and values determined for this purpose.
9. Discuss the different tests for the determination of pesticide residues and their significance.
10. Elaborate on the different ash values, their determination methods, and their importance in assessing the quality of crude drugs.

Answer Key for Multiple Choice Questions:

1. c) Science of Life
2. b) Kaumar Bhritya
3. c) Five
4. c) Dr. Samuel Hahnemann

5. d) Wood
6. c) Six
7. c) Arista and Asavas
8. c) Law of Maximum Potency
9. c) Mercury
10. d) Homoeopathy
11. a) Incineration.
12. a) Purification.
13. a) Lauha Bhasma.
14. c) It encourages microbial growth.
15. c) Foam test.
16. b) Quantity of Iodine absorbed by 100 g of the substance.
17. c) Neutralize the free acid.
18. b) Foam test.
19. c) Iodine test.
20. c) Purity.

CHAPTER - 4

NUTRACEUTICALS

"Nutraceuticals" is a broad term used to describe products derived from food sources that offer extra health benefits in addition to the basic nutritional value found in foods. They can be considered a bridge between food and pharmaceuticals. Nutraceuticals can be single compounds or may be products made up of multiple compounds, and they can be used as a part of a diet or consumed as dietary supplements, functional foods, or even in medicinal foods.

The word "nutraceutical" is a combination of "nutrition" and "pharmaceutical," coined to represent compounds that might have a potential therapeutic role. They may be useful in promoting health, preventing chronic diseases, delaying the aging process, or supporting the structure or function of the body.

NUTRACEUTICALS: OVERVIEW AND MARKET DETAILS

General Aspects:

1. **Definition:** As previously mentioned, nutraceuticals are products derived from food sources that provide additional health benefits beyond basic nutritional values.
2. **Categories:** They can be broadly classified into dietary supplements, functional foods, and medicinal foods.
3. **Benefits:** These products aim to prevent chronic diseases, improve health, delay the aging process, and enhance life expectancy.

Market and Growth:

1. **Size:** The global nutraceuticals market has been growing rapidly and is expected to continue to grow in the future. This growth is driven by rising health consciousness, aging populations, and increasing interest in preventive healthcare.
2. **Regions:** North America and Europe have been dominant players in the market, but the Asia-Pacific region, led by countries like China and India, is witnessing rapid growth due to increasing disposable income and awareness about health and wellness.
3. **Drivers:** Increased health awareness, a rising number of chronic diseases, a shift towards natural products, technological advancements, and evolving lifestyles are some factors propelling the market.

Scope:

1. **Prevention and Treatment:** Nutraceuticals cater to a range of health issues, from simple nutritional deficiencies to chronic conditions like cardiovascular diseases, diabetes, and cancer.
2. **R&D:** There's a considerable scope for research and development in nutraceuticals, especially in understanding the synergistic effects of food compounds, establishing more precise daily recommended intakes, and formulating products with enhanced bioavailability.

Types of Products Available in the Market:

1. **Dietary Supplements:** These are products taken orally that contain one or more dietary ingredients such as vitamins, minerals, amino acids, and herbs. Examples include multivitamin tablets, omega-3 capsules, and herbal supplements.
2. **Functional Foods:** These are foods that offer health benefits beyond basic nutrition. Examples include fortified cereals (with added vitamins and

minerals), probiotic yogurt, and foods fortified with plant sterols/stanols to lower cholesterol.

3. **Functional Beverages:** Drinks that offer health benefits. Examples include green tea (rich in antioxidants), energy drinks with added vitamins, and probiotic drinks.
4. **Medicinal Foods:** These are formulated to be consumed under the guidance of a physician and are intended for specific dietary management of a disease or condition. Examples might include meal replacements for patients with certain metabolic disorders.
5. **Specialty Nutraceuticals:** Products like probiotics, prebiotics, antioxidants, and polyunsaturated fatty acids fall under this category.

HEALTH BENEFITS AND ROLE OF NUTRACEUTICALS IN AILMENTS LIKE DIABETES, CVS DISEASES, CANCER, IRRITABLE BOWEL SYNDROME AND VARIOUS GASTRO INTESTINAL DISEASES

DIABETES:

Diabetes mellitus, commonly referred to simply as diabetes, is a chronic condition characterized by elevated blood sugar levels due to either an inability of the body to produce enough insulin (Type 1) or the body's decreased sensitivity to insulin (Type 2). Nutraceuticals can play a role in managing blood sugar levels, improving insulin sensitivity, and reducing the risk of complications associated with diabetes.

1. Alpha-lipoic acid (ALA):

a. Health Benefits: ALA is a potent antioxidant.

b. Role in Diabetes: It's been shown to improve insulin sensitivity and reduce the symptoms of peripheral neuropathy, a common complication of diabetes. Regular ALA supplementation can also reduce the oxidative stress that's often elevated in diabetes.

2. **Chromium:**
   a. Health Benefits: Chromium is an essential trace mineral.
   b. Role in Diabetes: It enhances the action of insulin in the body. Studies have suggested that chromium supplements might improve glucose metabolism and could be beneficial for people with insulin resistance.
3. **Cinnamon:**
   a. Health Benefits: Cinnamon is a common spice with antioxidant properties.
   b. Role in Diabetes: Some studies have found that cinnamon can lower blood sugar levels and improve insulin sensitivity. However, the evidence is mixed, and more research is needed to confirm these benefits.
4. **Bitter Melon:**
   a. Health Benefits: Bitter melon is a vegetable commonly used in traditional medicine.
   b. Role in Diabetes: It contains compounds that have insulin-like activity and can help in reducing blood sugar levels.
5. **Fenugreek:**
   a. Health Benefits: Fenugreek is a herb whose seeds are often used as a spice.
   b. Role in Diabetes: The seeds are rich in soluble fiber, which can help manage blood sugar levels. They might also improve glucose tolerance and insulin sensitivity.
6. **Omega-3 fatty acids:**
   a. **Health Benefits:** Omega-3s, especially eicosapentaenoic acid (EPA) and docosahexaenoic acid (DHA), have anti-inflammatory properties.

b. **Role in Diabetes:** Omega-3s can improve insulin sensitivity and reduce inflammation, which is beneficial for people with diabetes. They also help in reducing the risk of cardiovascular complications associated with diabetes.

7. **Berberine:**
   a. Health Benefits: Berberine is a compound found in several plants and has been used in traditional medicine.
   b. Role in Diabetes: It can activate an enzyme called AMPK, which regulates metabolism. Studies have shown that berberine can reduce blood sugar levels and improve insulin function.
8. **Magnesium:**
   a. Health Benefits: Magnesium is an essential mineral involved in various physiological processes.
   b. Role in Diabetes: A deficiency in magnesium can impair insulin function. Supplementing with magnesium can improve insulin sensitivity and control blood sugar levels.

CVS DISEASES

Cardiovascular diseases (CVDs) refer to a class of diseases that involve the heart or blood vessels, such as coronary artery disease, heart failure, and hypertension. Nutraceuticals can play a supportive role in managing, preventing, or reducing the risk factors associated with these diseases.

Cardiovascular Diseases (CVDs):

1. **Omega-3 fatty acids (EPA and DHA):**
   a. **Health Benefits:** Found in fatty fish and fish oil supplements, omega-3s have anti-inflammatory and antithrombotic properties.

   b. **Role in CVDs:** They can reduce triglyceride levels, decrease blood clotting, reduce blood pressure, and have been associated with a lower risk of sudden cardiac death and arrhythmias.

2. **Plant sterols and stanols:**
   a. **Health Benefits:** These compounds are found in small amounts in many grains, vegetables, fruits, legumes, nuts, and seeds.
   b. **Role in CVDs:** When consumed in larger, supplemented amounts, they can reduce LDL cholesterol levels by inhibiting its absorption in the intestines, which helps lower the risk of coronary heart disease.

3. **Coenzyme Q10 (CoQ10):**
   a. **Health Benefits:** An antioxidant that supports cellular energy production.
   b. **Role in CVDs:** It has been shown to improve endothelial function, reduce blood pressure, and is often recommended for patients taking statins (as these drugs can lower CoQ10 levels).

4. **Flavonoids:**
   a. **Health Benefits:** A diverse group of phytonutrients found in almost all fruits and vegetables. They have antioxidant, anti-inflammatory, and antiviral properties.
   b. **Role in CVDs:** They can improve endothelial function, reduce blood clotting, and lower blood pressure. Dark chocolate, berries, and green tea are particularly rich sources.

5. **L-arginine:**
   a. **Health Benefits:** An amino acid that's a precursor to nitric oxide, a molecule that helps blood vessels relax.
   b. **Role in CVDs:** Supplementation can improve vascular function and reduce blood pressure, though results vary among studies.

6. **Fiber:**

a. **Health Benefits**: Supports digestive health, reduces absorption of cholesterol.
b. **Role in CVDs:** Soluble fiber (like that found in oats, flaxseeds, and beans) can help reduce LDL cholesterol levels, thus reducing the risk of heart disease.

7. **Red yeast rice:**
   a. **Health Benefits:** Contains compounds similar to those found in statin drugs.
   b. **Role in CVDs:** It can help reduce LDL cholesterol levels. However, it's essential to use under medical supervision due to potential side effects and variability in potency.
8. **Garlic:**
   a. **Health Benefits:** Has antioxidant, anti-inflammatory, and antimicrobial properties.
   b. **Role in CVDs:** Some studies suggest that garlic can reduce blood pressure and cholesterol, helping in CVD prevention.
9. **Policosanols:**
   a. **Health Benefits:** Derived from the waxy coating of sugar cane.
   b. **Role in CVDs:** Some studies suggest it might help reduce LDL cholesterol levels.
10. **Magnesium:**
   a. **Health Benefits:** Essential for many cellular processes and reactions.
   b. **Role in CVDs:** It can help regulate blood pressure and has been associated with a reduced risk of CVDs.
11. **B Vitamins (especially B6, B12, and folic acid):**
   a. **Health Benefits:** Essential for many metabolic processes.

b. **Role in CVDs:** They can help reduce homocysteine levels, an amino acid linked to increased risk of cardiovascular diseases.

CANCER

Cancer is a group of diseases characterized by the uncontrolled growth and spread of abnormal cells. While nutraceuticals should not be viewed as a sole treatment for cancer, numerous compounds have shown potential anti-cancer properties or have been proposed to play supportive roles in cancer prevention and management.

Cancer:

1. **Curcumin (found in turmeric):**
   a. **Health Benefits:** Anti-inflammatory and antioxidant properties.
   b. **Role in Cancer:** Curcumin has shown promise in inhibiting the growth of various cancer cells in laboratory studies, reducing tumor growth, and potentiating the effects of chemotherapy.
2. **Green Tea Polyphenols (especially EGCG):**
   a. **Health Benefits:** Antioxidant properties.
   b. **Role in Cancer:** These compounds can inhibit tumor cell proliferation and induce apoptosis (programmed cell death). Epidemiological studies suggest that green tea consumption may reduce the risk of certain cancers.
3. **Sulforaphane (found in cruciferous vegetables like broccoli):**
   a. **Health Benefits:** Detoxification and antioxidant effects.
   b. **Role in Cancer:** It has been shown to inhibit the growth and induce apoptosis in cancer cells. It might also enhance the detoxification of certain carcinogens.
4. **Resveratrol (found in grapes, red wine, and peanuts):**
   a. **Health Benefits:** Anti-inflammatory and antioxidant properties.

b. **Role in Cancer:** It can inhibit the growth of cancer cells and activate apoptosis. It might also prevent tumor initiation, promotion, and progression.

5. **Lycopene (found in tomatoes):**
   a. **Health Benefits:** Antioxidant properties.
   b. **Role in Cancer:** Dietary intake of lycopene has been associated with a reduced risk of prostate and other cancers.
6. **Isoflavones (found in soy products):**
   a. **Health Benefits:** Antioxidant properties and hormonal effects.
   b. **Role in Cancer:** Some studies suggest a protective effect against breast and prostate cancers, but results are mixed. It's essential to consume in moderation.
7. **Indoles and Glucosinolates (found in cruciferous vegetables):**
   a. **Health Benefits:** Detoxification properties.
   b. **Role in Cancer:** These compounds help in the detoxification of carcinogens and may prevent DNA damage.
8. **Quercetin (found in onions, apples, and berries):**
   a. **Health Benefits:** Anti-inflammatory and antioxidant effects.
   b. **Role in Cancer:** It can inhibit tumor growth, reduce inflammation, and work synergistically with chemotherapy drugs to reduce their side effects.
9. **Omega-3 fatty acids:**
   a. **Health Benefits:** Anti-inflammatory properties.
   b. **Role in Cancer:** They can inhibit the growth of cancer cells, reduce inflammation, and potentiate the effects of chemotherapy.
10. **Modified Citrus Pectin:**
   a. **Health Benefits:** A type of soluble fiber.

b. **Role in Cancer:** It might inhibit cancer metastasis (spread) and reduce the growth of cancer cells.

11.Selenium:

a. **Health Benefits:** An essential trace mineral with antioxidant properties.

b. **Role in Cancer:** Supplementation has shown potential in reducing the risk of certain cancers, but excessive intake might be harmful.

Nutraceuticals have gained interest for their potential role in managing gastrointestinal (GI) disorders, including Irritable Bowel Syndrome (IBS) and other gastrointestinal diseases. While not a replacement for standard medical therapies, some of these compounds may offer symptom relief or even target some underlying causes.

IRRITABLE BOWEL SYNDROME AND VARIOUS GASTRO INTESTINAL DISEASES

1. Probiotic:

a. **Health Benefits:** They're beneficial bacteria that can support gut health.

b. **Role in GI Diseases:** Probiotics can enhance the gut barrier function, modulate the immune system, and compete with pathogenic bacteria. In IBS, specific strains might help reduce bloating, gas, and abdominal pain.

2. Prebiotics:

a. **Health Benefits:** Non-digestible fibers or compounds that feed beneficial gut bacteria.

b. **Role in GI Diseases:** They can support a healthy microbiota, leading to improved gut health and reduced symptoms, especially in functional bowel disorders.

3. Peppermint oil:

   a. **Health Benefits:** Antispasmodic effects.
   b. **Role in IBS:** Peppermint oil capsules can reduce abdominal pain in IBS by relaxing the intestinal muscles.
4. **Aloe vera:**
   a. **Health Benefits:** Anti-inflammatory and soothing properties.
   b. **Role in GI Diseases:** Consumed as a juice or gel, it can support healing in conditions like gastritis or ulcerative colitis. However, overconsumption can lead to diarrhea.
5. **Glutamine:**
   a. **Health Benefits:** An amino acid essential for the health of the intestinal lining.
   b. **Role in GI Diseases:** It can support the repair of the intestinal barrier, potentially beneficial in conditions like leaky gut syndrome or inflammatory bowel disease (IBD).
6. **Curcumin (found in turmeric):**
   a. **Health Benefits:** Anti-inflammatory properties.
   b. **Role in GI Diseases:** Curcumin can reduce inflammation in the gut and may be beneficial in conditions like ulcerative colitis or Crohn's disease.
7. **Fiber supplements (e.g., psyllium husk):**
   a. **Health Benefits:** Supports bowel regularity.
   b. **Role in IBS:** In IBS-C (constipation-predominant IBS), it can improve bowel movements and reduce abdominal pain.
8. **Digestive enzymes:**
   a. **Health Benefits:** Aid in breaking down food components.
   b. **Role in GI Diseases:** Helpful in conditions where there's a deficiency in natural enzyme production, such as pancreatitis or after gallbladder removal.

9. **Slippery Elm:**
   a. **Health Benefits:** Forms a soothing gel-like substance in the intestines.
   b. **Role in GI Diseases:** It can soothe the lining of the stomach and intestines, potentially helping conditions like gastritis or ulcerative colitis.

10. **Zinc-carnosine:**
   a. **Health Benefits:** Combines the mineral zinc and the di-peptide carnosine.
   b. **Role in GI Diseases:** It has antioxidant properties and can support the gut lining's health, especially in gastritis or when there's damage from non-steroidal anti-inflammatory drugs (NSAIDs).

11. **Ginger:**
   a. **Health Benefits:** Anti-nausea and some anti-inflammatory effects.
   b. **Role in GI Diseases**: Can be beneficial in nausea or an upset stomach.

12. **S. boulardii:** A probiotic yeast.
   a. **Health Benefits:** Anti-diarrheal properties.
   b. **Role in GI Diseases:** Often used to prevent antibiotic-associated diarrhea or treat conditions like Clostridium difficile infection.

STUDY OF HERBS AS HEALTH FOOD:

ALFAALFA

Alfalfa, sometimes known as lucerne in some parts of the world, is a perennial herb with a long history of use both as animal fodder and in human herbal medicine. Here's a look into alfalfa as a health food:

1. **Nutritional Profile:**
   a. Alfalfa is rich in vitamins, especially A, C, E, and K4. It also provides a variety of minerals including calcium, potassium, phosphorus, and iron.

b. It contains essential amino acids and is a source of protein, particularly when considered in the context of leafy greens.
c. Alfalfa also has dietary fiber, which can support digestive health.

2. **Health Benefits:**
    a. **Digestive Health:** Alfalfa has a high content of dietary fiber, which promotes bowel regularity and a healthy digestive system.
    b. **Cholesterol Reduction:** Some studies suggest that alfalfa can help lower cholesterol by binding to cholesterol molecules in the gut and preventing their absorption.
    c. **Antioxidant Properties:** Alfalfa contains various antioxidant compounds, which can help neutralize free radicals in the body, potentially reducing oxidative stress and the risk of chronic diseases.
    d. **Anti-inflammatory Properties:** Some compounds in alfalfa, like saponins, might have anti-inflammatory effects.
3. **Traditional Uses:**
    a. Historically, alfalfa has been used as an herbal medicine for various ailments, including kidney, bladder, and prostate conditions. It was also considered a tonic for digestive health.
    b. Some traditional systems of medicine use alfalfa to stimulate appetite and improve overall vigor and strength.
4. **Available Forms:**
    a. **Alfalfa Sprouts:** These are the young seedlings of the alfalfa plant and are commonly consumed in salads and sandwiches.
    b. **Alfalfa Tea:** Made from the dried leaves of the plant.
    c. **Alfalfa Supplements:** Available in capsules, tablets, or powders, often used by individuals looking for its health benefits in a concentrated form.
5. **Cautions:**

a. **Lupus (SLE):** There's some evidence that alfalfa might exacerbate symptoms of lupus or even trigger the disease in predisposed individuals due to its content of L-canavanine, an amino acid analog.
b. **Blood-thinning Medications:** Because of its high vitamin K content, alfalfa might interfere with the action of blood-thinning medications.
c. **Estrogenic Effects:** Alfalfa contains phytoestrogens, which can mimic the hormone estrogen in the body. While this can be beneficial in certain conditions, it's a consideration for individuals with hormone-sensitive conditions.

6. **Other Points:**
    a. While alfalfa is often considered safe for most people when consumed as a food, the concentrated forms (like supplements) should be approached with caution and ideally under the guidance of a healthcare professional.
    b. It's also worth noting that alfalfa fields are sometimes sprayed with chemicals or are genetically modified, so for those concerned about this, it's a good idea to choose organic alfalfa products.

CHICORY (CICHORIUM INTYBUS):

1. **Nutritional Profile:**
    a. Chicory root is a good source of inulin, a type of prebiotic fiber.
    b. It contains several vitamins and minerals, including zinc, magnesium, and potassium.
2. **Health Benefits:**
    a. **Digestive Health:** The inulin in chicory root acts as food for beneficial bacteria in the gut, promoting a healthier gut microbiome.
    b. **Blood Sugar Regulation:** The inulin in chicory might help stabilize blood sugar levels.

c. **Cholesterol:** Some studies suggest chicory can help reduce LDL cholesterol.
d. **Liver Health:** Chicory has traditionally been used to detoxify the liver.

3. **Traditional Uses:**
   a. Chicory has been used as a coffee substitute or additive, especially in parts of Europe. The root is roasted and ground and has a taste somewhat similar to coffee but is caffeine-free.
   b. Traditionally used in herbal medicine as a digestive tonic and liver cleanser.
4. **Available Forms:**
   a. **Chicory Coffee:** Roasted chicory root used alone or blended with coffee.
   b. **Chicory Root Extract:** Often used in supplements or as an ingredient in certain foods.
   c. **Fresh Chicory Leaves:** Used in salads and have a slightly bitter taste.
5. **Cautions:**
   a. Large amounts of chicory root can cause bloating, gas, and other digestive symptoms due to its high inulin content.
   b. Those allergic to ragweed and related plants might also be allergic to chicory.

GINGER (ZINGIBER OFFICINALE):

1. **Nutritional Profile:**
   a. Contains gingerol, a substance with powerful medicinal properties.
   b. Provides vitamin B6, magnesium, phosphorus, zinc, folate, riboflavin, and niacin.
2. **Health Benefits:**

a. **Nausea Relief:** Ginger can treat nausea related to pregnancy, chemotherapy, and surgery.
b. **Digestive Health:** Helps soothe digestive disturbances and can enhance gastric motility.
c. **Anti-inflammatory and Antioxidant Effects:** Gingerol in ginger can help reduce oxidative stress and inflammation in the body.
d. **Pain Reduction:** Some studies suggest ginger can reduce muscle pain and soreness.
e. **Chronic Diseases:** Ginger might have protective effects against cancer, diabetes, and cardiovascular diseases due to its anti-inflammatory and antioxidative properties.

3. **Traditional Uses:**
    a. Ginger has been used for thousands of years in various cultures for its medicinal properties.
    b. Commonly used to treat digestive disturbances and as a warming remedy.
4. **Available Forms:**
    a. **Fresh Ginger Root:** Can be sliced, minced, or grated and used in cooking or made into tea.
    b. **Dried Ginger:** Used as a spice in cooking and baking.
    c. **Ginger Supplements:** Available in capsules, tablets, or extracts.
    d. **Ginger Essential Oil:** Used in aromatherapy and topical treatments.
5. **Cautions:**
    a. High doses of ginger can cause digestive upset.
    b. Ginger might interfere with blood-thinning medications due to its antiplatelet effects.
    c. Some individuals might be allergic or sensitive to ginger.

FENUGREEK (TRIGONELLA FOENUM-GRAECUM):

1. **Nutritional Profile:**
   a. Fenugreek seeds are a rich source of protein, dietary fiber, B vitamins, iron, and several other minerals.
   b. They contain phytonutrients like choline and various beneficial alkaloids.
2. **Health Benefits:**
   a. **Blood Sugar Control:** Fenugreek seeds have been studied for their role in blood sugar management, making them beneficial for people with diabetes.
   b. **Cholesterol Regulation:** They can help reduce LDL ("bad") cholesterol levels.
   c. **Digestive Health:** The fiber in fenugreek aids digestion and can relieve constipation.
   d. **Milk Production:** Fenugreek has been traditionally used to increase milk production in breastfeeding mothers.
   e. **Anti-inflammatory Properties:** Compounds in fenugreek may reduce inflammation in the body.
3. **Traditional Uses:**
   a. Used as a spice in many cuisines, especially in Indian and Middle Eastern dishes.
   b. It has been used in Ayurveda and traditional medicine for its therapeutic properties.
4. **Available Forms:**
   a. **Seeds:** Used as a spice or can be sprouted.
   b. **Powder:** Ground seeds used in cooking or as a supplement.
   c. **Tea:** Made from steeping the seeds.
   d. **Capsules:** For those seeking concentrated health benefits.

5. Cautions:
    a. In high doses, fenugreek can cause digestive distress.
    b. Pregnant women should avoid consuming large amounts as fenugreek might stimulate uterine contractions.

GARLIC (ALLIUM SATIVUM):

1. **Nutritional Profile:**
    a. Contains vitamins C and B6, manganese, selenium, and other antioxidants.
    b. Allicin, a compound produced when garlic is crushed or chopped, has medicinal properties.
2. **Health Benefits:**
    a. **Cardiovascular Health:** Garlic has been linked to reduced blood pressure and lower cholesterol, making it beneficial for heart health.
    b. **Immune Support:** Regular consumption can boost the immune system and help fight common illnesses.
    c. **Antibacterial and Antiviral:** Garlic has natural microbial properties.
    d. **Cancer Prevention:** Some studies suggest garlic consumption may reduce the risk of certain types of cancer.
    e. **Detoxification:** Garlic can help detoxify heavy metals in the body.
3. **Traditional Uses:**
    a. Widely used as a flavoring in cooking due to its strong aroma and delicious taste.
    b. Has been used in traditional medicine for centuries to treat ailments ranging from the common cold to parasites.
4. **Available Forms:**

a. **Raw Cloves:** Can be eaten raw, cooked, or used to flavor dishes.
b. **Powder or Granules:** Used in cooking or as a supplement.
c. **Capsules:** Garlic supplements are available for those seeking its health benefits without the strong taste.
d. **Oil:** Used for cooking or in natural health remedies.

5. **Cautions:**
    a. Consuming large amounts of garlic, especially on an empty stomach, can lead to digestive issues.
    b. Can interfere with certain medications, especially blood-thinners.
    c. Some people may experience an allergic reaction or skin irritation from handling or consuming garlic.

HONEY:

1. **Nutritional Profile:**
    a. Honey contains natural sugars (mostly fructose and glucose), as well as trace amounts of vitamins, minerals, amino acids, and antioxidants.
    b. Darker honey varieties generally have more antioxidants and minerals than lighter ones.
2. **Health Benefits:**
    a. **Antibacterial and Antimicrobial:** Honey can inhibit bacterial growth, making it beneficial for wound healing.
    b. **Soothing Throat:** It can provide relief from sore throats and coughs.
    c. **Digestive Health:** Honey can help treat digestive issues like diarrhea, though the evidence is not robust.
    d. **Antioxidant Properties:** It contains phenolic compounds, flavonoids, and enzymes that combat oxidative stress.

3. **Traditional Uses:**
    a. Used as a natural sweetener in many cultures.
    b. Traditionally applied to wounds, burns, and skin conditions for its healing properties.
4. **Cautions:**
    a. Raw honey can contain botulism spores, so it should not be given to infants under 12 months old.
    b. Some people may have an allergic reaction to specific components in honey.

AMLA (INDIAN GOOSEBERRY, PHYLLANTHUS EMBLICA):

1. **Nutritional Profile:**
    a. Rich in vitamin C, which is a powerful antioxidant.
    b. Contains other vitamins and minerals, including calcium, phosphorus, iron, carotene, and vitamin B complex.
2. **Health Benefits:**
    a. **Immune Booster:** Due to its high vitamin C content, Amla can boost the immune system.
    b. **Hair and Skin Health:** Often used in hair tonics and skincare products.
    c. **Digestive Health:** Amla can aid digestion and help prevent constipation.
    d. **Anti-inflammatory:** Helps in reducing inflammation in the body.
    e. **Blood Sugar Control:** Can help regulate blood sugar levels.
3. **Traditional Uses:**
    a. Widely used in Ayurvedic medicine for a variety of ailments.
    b. A key ingredient in 'Triphala', a traditional Ayurvedic formulation.
4. **Cautions:**

a. Consumed in large amounts, Amla might increase the risk of bleeding or lower blood sugar levels too much, especially in combination with diabetes medications.

GINSENG:

1. **Nutritional Profile:**
    a. Contains ginsenosides, the primary active compounds of ginseng.
    b. Provides a variety of vitamins, minerals, and antioxidants.
2. **Health Benefits:**
    a. **Cognitive Function:** May improve mental clarity and reduce fatigue.
    b. **Immune System:** Some studies suggest ginseng can boost the immune system.
    c. **Stress Reduction:** Recognized as an adaptogen, helping the body adapt to stress.
    d. **Blood Sugar Control:** Ginseng has shown potential benefits for controlling blood sugar in people with and without diabetes.
3. **Traditional Uses:**
    a. Widely used in traditional Chinese medicine for thousands of years to boost energy and overall health.
    b. Consumed as tea, soup, or in extract form.
4. **Cautions:**
    a. Can interact with certain medications, including those for diabetes, depression, and high blood pressure.
    b. Some people may experience side effects like headaches, insomnia, or digestive problems.

ASHWAGANDHA (WITHANIA SOMNIFERA):

1. **Nutritional Profile:**
    a. Contains withanolides, the primary active compounds associated with its medicinal properties.
    b. Other constituents include alkaloids, choline, fatty acids, amino acids, and a variety of sugars.
2. **Health Benefits:**
    a. **Stress and Anxiety:** Recognized as an adaptogen, Ashwagandha helps the body adapt to stress and has been shown to reduce cortisol levels and alleviate symptoms of stress and anxiety.
    b. **Cognitive Function:** Might enhance brain function, memory, reaction times, and the ability to perform tasks.
    c. **Antioxidant and Anti-inflammatory:** Contains components that can help reduce inflammation and oxidative stress in the body.
    d. **Blood Sugar Control:** Some studies indicate it can reduce blood sugar levels.
    e. **Thyroid Function:** Can influence thyroid hormone levels, potentially benefiting those with thyroid disorders.
3. **Traditional Uses:**
    a. A staple of Ayurvedic medicine, it's often referred to as "Indian ginseng."
    b. Used to boost vitality, improve overall health, and promote longevity.
4. **Cautions:**
    a. Might cause mild side effects such as drowsiness, gastrointestinal discomfort, or headaches in some individuals.
    b. Should be used cautiously by those with thyroid conditions or those on thyroid medication.

SPIRULINA (ARTHROSPIRA PLATENSIS AND ARTHROSPIRA MAXIMA):

1. **Nutritional Profile:**
    a. A type of blue-green algae that's incredibly protein-rich (about 60%-70% of its dry weight).
    b. Contains a range of vitamins and minerals, including B vitamins, iron, and manganese.
    c. Provides a unique pigment called phycocyanin, which has antioxidant properties.
2. **Health Benefits:**
    a. **Nutrient-Rich:** Offers essential amino acids, making it a popular protein source for vegetarians and vegans.
    b. **Antioxidant and Anti-inflammatory:** Phycocyanin not only gives Spirulina its blue-green color but also has antioxidant and anti-inflammatory properties.
    c. **Cholesterol and Blood Pressure:** Some studies suggest it can reduce LDL cholesterol and may lower blood pressure.
    d. **Blood Sugar Control:** May help reduce blood sugar levels.
    e. **Boosted Immune Function:** Spirulina can enhance the production of antibodies and promote increased immune system activity.
3. **Traditional Uses:**
    a. Used as a food source by ancient civilizations, including the Aztecs.
    b. Harvested from freshwater lakes, ponds, and rivers, then dried into cakes or powder.
4. **Cautions:**

a. Contaminated Spirulina can be harmful, so it's essential to ensure it's sourced from a reputable producer to avoid contaminants or heavy metals.

b. Might cause mild digestive upset in some individuals.

Multiple Choice Questions:

1. What term is used to describe products derived from food sources that offer extra health benefits in addition to the basic nutritional value found in foods?

   a. Pharmaceuticals

   b. Nutrients

   c. Nutraceuticals

   d. Superfoods

2. What are the two words combined to form the term "nutraceutical"?

   a. Nutrient and Pharmaceutical

   b. Natural and Chemical

   c. Nutrition and Pharmaceutical

   d. Nutty and Practical

3. Which region is witnessing rapid growth in the nutraceuticals market due to increasing disposable income and awareness about health and wellness?

   a. North America

   b. Europe

   c. Asia-Pacific

   d. Africa

4. Which of the following is NOT a type of product available in the nutraceuticals market?

   a. Dietary Supplements

   b. Functional Beverages

c. Medicinal Tablets

d. Medicinal Foods

5. Which compound in turmeric shows potential anti-cancer properties?

   a. Lycopene

   b. Curcumin

   c. EGCG

   d. Sulforaphane

6. What does the term "Adaptogen" mean?

   a. A compound that helps the body produce more energy

   b. A compound that helps the body adapt to stress

   c. A compound that helps the body fight infections

   d. A compound that helps in digestion

7. Which compound is responsible for the medicinal properties of garlic?

   a. Gingerol

   b. Curcumin

   c. Allicin

   d. Ginsenosides

8. Fenugreek seeds are particularly rich in which type of dietary component?

   a. Carbohydrates

   b. Fats

   c. Proteins

   d. Sugars

9. What is the potential harmful effect of giving raw honey to infants under 12 months old?

   a. High sugar content

   b. Allergic reactions

   c. Botulism spores

d. Indigestion

10. Which of the following is NOT a traditional use of ginseng?

a. Boosting energy

b. Treating cold

c. Increasing appetite

d. Treating insomnia

11. Which compound in fenugreek might help in blood sugar management?

a. Withanolides

b. Allicin

c. Ginsenosides

d. Inulin

12. What is the major protein source in Spirulina?

a. Phycocyanin

b. Curcumin

c. Ginsenosides

d. Blue-green algae

13. Which compound found in cinnamon can lower blood sugar levels and improve insulin sensitivity?

a. Gingerol

b. Curcumin

c. Allicin

d. Cinnamaldehyde

14. Which of the following is a health benefit of Omega-3 fatty acids in diabetes?

a. Reduce inflammation

b. Increase blood sugar levels

c. Decrease insulin sensitivity

d. Increase oxidative stress

15. Which vitamin is particularly abundant in Amla (Indian Gooseberry)?

a. Vitamin A

b. Vitamin B

c. Vitamin C

d. Vitamin D

16. Which of the following is NOT a traditional use of Ashwagandha?

a. Boost vitality

b. Improve hair growth

c. Improve overall health

d. Promote longevity

17. What component in chicory root acts as food for beneficial bacteria in the gut?

a. Ginsenosides

b. Inulin

c. Allicin

d. Curcumin

18. Which compound found in broccoli can inhibit the growth and induce apoptosis in cancer cells?

a. Curcumin

b. Gingerol

c. Sulforaphane

d. Allicin

19. Which herb is known to increase milk production in breastfeeding mothers?

a. Ginseng

b. Fenugreek

c. Ginger

d. Amla

20. Which component of alfalfa might exacerbate symptoms of lupus?

a. Allicin

b. Ginsenosides

c. L-canavanine

d. Curcumin

Short Answer Type Questions (Subjective):

1. What is the definition of nutraceuticals?
2. List the three broad classifications of nutraceuticals.
3. How do nutraceuticals aim to enhance life expectancy?
4. Name two regions that have been dominant players in the nutraceuticals market.
5. What role does ALA play in diabetes management?
6. How can cinnamon potentially benefit diabetic patients?
7. How do Omega-3 fatty acids benefit individuals with cardiovascular diseases?
8. Name one source of flavonoids beneficial for cardiovascular health.
9. What compound in turmeric has shown potential anti-cancer properties?
10. How does green tea potentially reduce the risk of certain cancers?
11. How do probiotics benefit gastrointestinal diseases?
12. Which herb is known for its antispasmodic effects in treating IBS?
13. What are the potential health benefits of alfalfa?
14. Why is chicory considered beneficial for digestive health?
15. What are the main active compounds of ginseng?
16. How does Ashwagandha help the body adapt to stress?
17. Why is spirulina popular among vegetarians and vegans?
18. What is the unique pigment in spirulina with antioxidant properties?
19. Name the compound in garlic that is produced when it is crushed or chopped.
20. How does fenugreek potentially benefit individuals with diabetes?

Long Answer Type Questions (Subjective):

1. Explain the difference between dietary supplements, functional foods, and medicinal foods, providing examples for each.
2. Discuss the scope and potential areas of research and development in nutraceuticals.
3. Describe the various benefits of Omega-3 fatty acids in managing diabetes and cardiovascular diseases.
4. Elaborate on the potential anti-cancer properties of green tea polyphenols and sulforaphane.
5. Discuss the traditional and contemporary uses of ginger in promoting health.
6. Explain the role of nutraceuticals in managing gastrointestinal disorders, including IBS.
7. Discuss the nutritional profile, health benefits, traditional uses, and cautions associated with ginseng.
8. Describe the potential benefits and traditional uses of honey as a health food.
9. Elaborate on the health benefits and potential risks associated with consuming alfalfa.
10. Discuss the significance of the nutraceuticals market in today's health-conscious society, focusing on its growth drivers and regional dynamics.

Answer Key of Multiple Choice Questions :

1. c. Nutraceuticals
2. c. Nutrition and Pharmaceutical
3. c. Asia-Pacific
4. c. Medicinal Tablets
5. b. Curcumin
6. b. A compound that helps the body adapt to stress

7. c. Allicin
8. c. Proteins
9. c. Botulism spores
10. d. Treating insomnia
11. d. Inulin
12. d. Blue-green algae
13. d. Cinnamaldehyde
14. a. Reduce inflammation
15. c. Vitamin C
16. b. Improve hair growth
17. b. Inulin
18. c. Sulforaphane
19. b. Fenugreek
20. c. L-canavanine

CHAPTER - 5

HERBAL-DRUG AND HERB-FOOD INTERACTIONS

INTRODUCTION

Interactions between herbal remedies, pharmaceutical drugs, and food are important considerations in healthcare. These interactions can have various effects on drug effectiveness, safety, and overall health. Understanding these interactions is crucial for healthcare professionals and individuals using herbal remedies or medications. Here's a general introduction to the interactions and their classification, along with examples:

1. Herbal-Drug Interactions: Herbal-drug interactions occur when herbal remedies affect the pharmacokinetics (absorption, distribution, metabolism, excretion) or pharmacodynamics (effects) of pharmaceutical drugs. These interactions can result in various outcomes:

a. **Potentiation:** The herbal remedy enhances the effects of the drug, potentially leading to overdose or increased side effects.

b. **Antagonism:** The herbal remedy reduces the effects of the drug, diminishing its efficacy.

c. **Alteration of Drug Metabolism:** Some herbs can affect drug metabolism in the liver, leading to changes in drug concentrations in the bloodstream.

d. **Adverse Effects**: Interactions can result in adverse effects, including toxicity or reduced therapeutic benefits.

Examples of Herbal-Drug Interactions:

i. **St. John's Wort (Hypericum perforatum):** Interacts with various medications, including antidepressants, oral contraceptives, and anticoagulants. It can reduce the effectiveness of these drugs.
ii. **Ginkgo Biloba:** May interact with blood-thinning medications like aspirin and warfarin, increasing the risk of bleeding.
iii. **Garlic:** Can enhance the effects of anticoagulant drugs, potentially increasing the risk of bleeding.
iv. **Echinacea:** May interact with immunosuppressive drugs, affecting their efficacy.
v. **Grapefruit:** Not an herb but commonly consumed with medications, especially statins, leading to altered drug metabolism.

2. Herb-Food Interactions: Herb-food interactions refer to the effects of consuming herbs alongside specific foods, impacting the absorption, bioavailability, or effectiveness of herbal remedies. Food can influence the gastrointestinal tract's physiology and metabolic processes, leading to various outcomes:

a. **Enhanced Absorption:** Some foods can increase the absorption of specific herbal compounds.
b. **Reduced Absorption:** Certain foods can decrease the absorption of herbal components.
c. **Altered Metabolism:** Food can affect the metabolism of herbal compounds, influencing their bioavailability and duration of action.

Examples of Herb-Food Interactions:

i. **Turmeric:** Consuming turmeric with black pepper enhances the absorption of its active compound, curcumin.

ii. **Milk Thistle:** Taking milk thistle with a high-fat meal may improve the absorption of its active constituents, silymarin.

iii. **Green Tea:** Some foods and beverages, like dairy products, can bind to the catechins in green tea, potentially reducing their bioavailability.

CLASSIFICATION OF INTERACTIONS:

1. **Pharmacokinetic Interactions:**
   a. Affect the absorption, distribution, metabolism, or excretion of drugs or herbs.
   b. **Example:** St. John's Wort induces the cytochrome P450 enzyme system, accelerating the metabolism of various drugs.
2. **Pharmacodynamic Interactions:**
   a. Alter the effects of drugs or herbs on the body.
   b. **Example:** Ginkgo Biloba, used alongside blood-thinning medications, can increase the risk of bleeding due to its antiplatelet effects.
3. **Pharmaceutical Interactions:**
   a. Occur when herbal remedies interfere with the formulation or stability of pharmaceutical drugs.
   b. **Example:** Some herbs can affect the dissolution of drug tablets or capsules.
4. **Nutrient Interactions:**
   a. Certain herbs or supplements can lead to imbalances in nutrient levels in the body, potentially affecting overall health.
   b. **Example:** Excessive use of licorice root can lead to potassium depletion.

STUDY OF DRUGS AND THEIR POSSIBLE SIDE EFFECTS AND INTERACTIONS:

Here's a brief overview of the mentioned drugs (most of which are herbal supplements), their potential side effects, and known interactions:

1. Hypericum (St. John's Wort)

Possible Side Effects:

1. Dry mouth
2. Dizziness
3. Diarrhea
4. Nausea
5. Increased sensitivity to sunlight
6. Fatigue

Known Interactions:

1. Antidepressants: Can lead to a potentially life-threatening increase in serotonin.
2. Oral contraceptives: May reduce the effectiveness of birth control pills.
3. Anticoagulants: Can reduce the effectiveness of these drugs.
4. HIV drugs: May reduce the effectiveness of antiretroviral drugs.

2. Kava-Kava

Possible Side Effects:

1. Liver damage or failure
2. Dizziness
3. Fatigue
4. Dry, scaly skin
5. Stomach pain

Known Interactions:

1. Alcohol: Increases the risk of liver damage.
2. Sedative medications: Can enhance the sedative effects, increasing the risk of excessive sedation.

3. Ginkgo Biloba

Possible Side Effects:

1. Headaches
2. Dizziness
3. Heart palpitations
4. Upset stomach
5. Skin reactions

Known Interactions:

1. Blood thinners: Can increase the risk of bleeding.
2. Anticonvulsants: Might reduce the effectiveness of seizure medications.

4. Ginseng

Possible Side Effects:

1. Headaches
2. Sleep disturbances
3. Diarrhea
4. Mania in people with depression
5. Rapid heartbeat

Known Interactions:

1. Blood thinners: Can increase the risk of bleeding.
2. Stimulants: Can increase the effects and side effects of caffeine and other stimulants.
3. Diabetic medication: Might lower blood sugar, altering the effects of diabetes medications.

5. Garlic

Possible Side Effects:

1. Breath and body odor
2. Heartburn
3. Upset stomach

4. Allergic reactions

Known Interactions:

1. Blood thinners: Can increase the risk of bleeding.
2. HIV drugs: Garlic can lower the body's levels of certain HIV drugs.

6. Pepper (Assuming Black Pepper)

Possible Side Effects:

1. Stomach upset
2. Burning aftertaste

Known Interactions:

Medications metabolized by the liver: Black pepper might increase how quickly some medications are changed and broken down by the liver.

7. Ephedra (Ma Huang)

Possible Side Effects:

1. High blood pressure
2. Increased heart rate
3. Nervousness
4. Sleep disturbances
5. Severe skin reactions
6. Urinary retention

Known Interactions:

1. Stimulants: Increases the stimulant effects, raising blood pressure and heart rate.
2. MAOI antidepressants: Can lead to dangerous side effects like rapid heart rate and high blood pressure.
3. Theophylline: May increase the risk of side effects from theophylline.

It's crucial to note that anyone considering using these herbs (or any supplement) should consult with a healthcare professional first. The effects can vary based on individual health, the presence of other medications, and other factors.

Multiple Choice Questions (MCQs):

1. Herbal-drug interactions occur when:
   a. Herbal remedies affect only the pharmacodynamics of pharmaceutical drugs.
   b. Herbal remedies affect only the pharmacokinetics of pharmaceutical drugs.
   c. Herbal remedies affect both the pharmacodynamics and pharmacokinetics of pharmaceutical drugs.
   d. Herbal remedies have no effect on pharmaceutical drugs.
2. Which of the following describes the outcome of potentiation in herbal-drug interactions?
   a. Herbal remedy enhances the effects of the drug.
   b. Herbal remedy reduces the effects of the drug.
   c. Herbal remedy alters drug metabolism in the liver.
   d. Herbal remedy has no effect on the drug.
3. St. John's Wort interacts with which of the following medications?
   a. Antihistamines
   b. Antibiotics
   c. Anticoagulants
   b. Antipyretics
4. Ginkgo Biloba, when taken with specific medications, can increase the risk of:
   a. Hypertension
   b. Insomnia
   c. Bleeding
   d. Nausea

5. Grapefruit commonly interacts with:
   a. Antipyretics
   b. Statins
   c. Diuretics
   d. Antacids
6. The consumption of which herb with black pepper enhances the absorption of its active compound?
   a. Ginger
   b. Garlic
   c. Green Tea
   d. Turmeric
7. Pharmacokinetic interactions affect:
   a. Only the absorption of drugs or herbs.
   b. Only the metabolism of drugs or herbs.
   c. Both the absorption and metabolism of drugs or herbs.
   d. The effects of drugs or herbs on the body.
8. What does Ginkgo Biloba's antiplatelet effect result in when used with blood-thinning medications?
   a. Pharmacokinetic interaction
   b. Pharmacodynamic interaction
   c. Pharmaceutical interaction
   d. Nutrient interaction
9. Which of the following herbs can lead to potassium depletion when used excessively?
   a. Milk Thistle
   b. Turmeric
   c. Licorice root

d. Echinacea

10.Herb-food interactions can:

a. Only enhance the absorption of herbal compounds.

b. Only reduce the absorption of herbal compounds.

c. Both enhance and reduce the absorption of herbal compounds.

d. Have no effect on the absorption of herbal compounds.

11.Which of the following drugs can lead to an increased sensitivity to sunlight?

a. Kava-Kava

b. Ginkgo Biloba

c. Hypericum (St. John's Wort)

d. Ginseng

12.What is a potential side effect of Ginseng?

a. Breath and body odor

b. Mania in people with depression

c. Dry, scaly skin

d. Stomach upset

13.Which drug might reduce the effectiveness of antiretroviral drugs?

a. Garlic

b. Pepper

c. Hypericum (St. John's Wort)

d. Ephedra

14.Kava-Kava's interaction with which of the following can enhance sedative effects?

a. Blood thinners

b. Sedative medications

c. HIV drugs

d. Stimulants

15.Which drug can potentially increase the risk of bleeding when taken with blood thinners?

a. Ginkgo Biloba

b. Kava-Kava

c. Ephedra

d. Hypericum

16.Which of the following might be altered by Ginseng?

a. Blood pressure and heart rate

b. Liver function

c. Blood sugar levels

d. Sensitivity to sunlight

17.Ephedra can lead to dangerous side effects when combined with:

a. Anticonvulsants

b. HIV drugs

c. MAOI antidepressants

d. Sedative medications

18.Which drug's possible side effect includes "Liver damage or failure"?

a. Garlic

b. Ginkgo Biloba

c. Kava-Kava

d. Hypericum

19.Black pepper may affect the metabolism of medications processed by:

a. Kidneys

b. Heart

c. Lungs

d. Liver

20.A potential side effect of Garlic is:

a. Increased heart rate

b. Breath and body odor

c. Severe skin reactions

d. Sleep disturbances

Short Answer Type Questions (Subjective):

1. Explain the difference between pharmacokinetics and pharmacodynamics.
2. How can Echinacea affect the efficacy of immunosuppressive drugs?
3. Describe the impact of food on the absorption of the active constituents of Milk Thistle.
4. What is the significance of the interaction between Turmeric and black pepper?
5. How can herbal remedies interfere with the formulation or stability of pharmaceutical drugs?
6. Describe the potential side effects of Hypericum (St. John's Wort).
7. What are the known interactions of Ephedra (Ma Huang)?
8. How can Ginseng affect people with diabetes?
9. Why should someone consuming Kava-Kava be cautious when drinking alcohol?
10. How might black pepper influence the metabolism of certain medications?

Long Answer Type Questions (Subjective):

1. Discuss the various outcomes of herbal-drug interactions and provide examples for each.
2. Describe the potential risks and benefits of herb-food interactions, citing specific examples.
3. Elaborate on the different classifications of interactions and provide examples illustrating each type.

4. Discuss the significance of understanding interactions between herbal remedies, pharmaceutical drugs, and food in healthcare.
5. Explain the potential adverse effects that can result from herbal-drug interactions and the precautions that should be taken.
6. Discuss the side effects and interactions of Ginkgo Biloba, highlighting its potential dangers and benefits.
7. Explain the significance of interactions between herbal remedies and other medications, using the provided drugs as examples.
8. Describe the potential health implications of consuming Hypericum and its interactions with various medications.
9. Discuss the importance of consulting with a healthcare professional before using herbal supplements, especially in the context of the drugs mentioned.
10. Explore the side effects and interactions of Ginseng, emphasizing its effects on mental health and blood sugar levels.

Answer Key for Multiple Choice Questions:

1. c. Herbal remedies affect both the pharmacodynamics and pharmacokinetics of pharmaceutical drugs.
2. a. Herbal remedy enhances the effects of the drug.
3. c. Anticoagulants
4. c. Bleeding
5. b. Statins
6. d. Turmeric
7. c. Both the absorption and metabolism of drugs or herbs.
8. b. Pharmacodynamic interaction
9. c. Licorice root
10. c. Both enhance and reduce the absorption of herbal compounds.

11.c. Hypericum (St. John's Wort)
12.b. Mania in people with depression
13.c. Hypericum (St. John's Wort)
14.b. Sedative medications
15.a. Ginkgo Biloba
16.c. Blood sugar levels
17.c. MAOI antidepressants
18.c. Kava-Kava
19.d. Liver
20.b. Breath and body odor

CHAPTER - 6

HERBAL COSMETICS

Herbal Cosmetics refer to cosmetic products formulated using various permissible herbal ingredients to have therapeutic benefits, enhancing beauty or appearance. These cosmetics utilize the natural properties of herbs, a practice rooted in ancient traditions from cultures worldwide.

The word 'cosmetics' arises from a Greek word 'kosmeticos' which means to adorn. Since that time ant material used for beautification or improvement of appearance is known as cosmetics.

CLASSIFICATION OF COSMETICS:

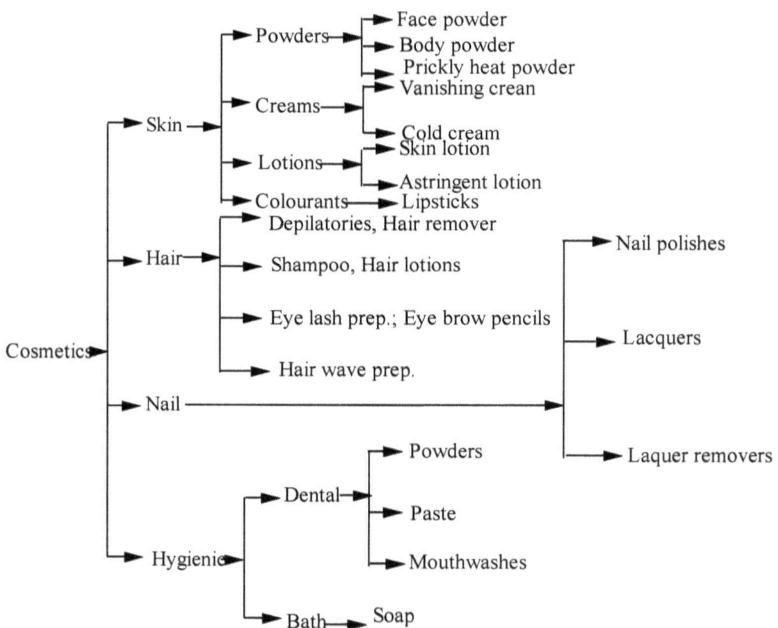

CHARACTERISTICS AND COMPONENTS OF HERBAL COSMETICS:

1. **Natural Ingredients:** Herbal cosmetics are generally formulated using components derived from plants such as leaves, roots, stems, flowers, and seeds. These might include aloe vera, turmeric, neem, tulsi (holy basil), saffron, and various essential oils, among others.
2. **Therapeutic Properties**: Beyond cosmetic enhancement, many herbal cosmetics claim to offer therapeutic properties such as anti-acne, anti-wrinkle, skin revitalizing, anti-dandruff, hair strengthening, etc.
3. **Safety and Hypoallergenic Traits:** Herbal cosmetics often promote themselves as safer alternatives to synthetic products, asserting fewer side effects or allergic reactions. However, this doesn't mean they're entirely devoid of allergic risks—individual reactions to natural ingredients can still occur.
4. **Eco-friendly:** As they primarily utilize natural ingredients, herbal cosmetics often position themselves as environmentally friendly. This attribute aligns with an increasing consumer demand for sustainable and eco-friendly products.
5. **Comprehensive Range:** The range of herbal cosmetics includes skincare products (creams, lotions, face packs, masks), haircare products (shampoos, oils, conditioners), make-up products, fragrances, and more.

ADVANTAGES OF HERBAL COSMETICS:

1. **Fewer Chemicals:** Herbal cosmetics usually have fewer synthetic chemicals, which some consumers believe reduces the risk of skin irritations or allergies.
2. **Nutrient-Rich:** Many natural ingredients used in herbal cosmetics are rich in antioxidants, vitamins, and essential oils that can nourish the skin or hair.
3. **Holistic Approach:** Herbal products often adopt a holistic approach to beauty, aiming to enhance overall health and well-being along with cosmetic benefits.

CONCERNS AND CONSIDERATIONS:

1. **Efficacy:** While many herbal cosmetics have proven benefits, the efficacy of others might be anecdotal. Consumers should approach claims critically and seek evidence-based results.
2. **Regulation:** The regulation of herbal cosmetics varies by country, and not all products undergo rigorous testing. This inconsistency can affect product quality and safety.
3. **Preservation:** Natural products without preservatives may have a shorter shelf life. Some herbal cosmetics might incorporate natural preservatives, but their effectiveness in comparison to synthetic alternatives can vary.

SOURCES AND DESCRIPTION OF RAW MATERIALS OF HERBAL ORIGIN USED VIA, FIXED OILS

Fixed oils, often referred to as "carrier oils" in the context of herbal medicine and aromatherapy, are typically derived from the seeds, nuts, or fruits of plants. Unlike essential oils, which are volatile and can evaporate, fixed oils do not evaporate and remain "fixed" on the skin or surface. Here are some commonly used fixed oils, their sources, and a brief description:

1. **Olive Oil (Olea europaea)**
   a. **Source:** Extracted from the fruit of the olive tree.
   b. **Description:** Olive oil is rich in monounsaturated fatty acids and has various uses, from culinary to skincare. It's known for its moisturizing properties and is commonly used in massage and skincare formulations.
2. **Coconut Oil (Cocos nucifera)**
   a. **Source:** Derived from the meat or kernel of the coconut fruit.

b. **Description:** Coconut oil solidifies at cooler temperatures but melts easily on the skin. It has moisturizing properties and is often used in skincare and haircare products.

3. **Almond Oil (Prunus dulcis)**
   a. **Source:** Extracted from the kernels of sweet almonds.
   b. **Description:** Almond oil is light, easily absorbed by the skin, and is often used as a base for massage oils and skin creams.
4. **Jojoba Oil (Simmondsia chinensis)**
   a. **Source:** Derived from the seeds of the jojoba plant.
   b. **Description:** Technically a liquid wax, jojoba oil resembles human sebum closely. It's great for balancing oil in the skin and is commonly used in skincare products.
5. **Grapeseed Oil (Vitis vinifera)**
   a. **Source:** Extracted from grape seeds, often a byproduct of winemaking.
   b. **Description:** Grapeseed oil is lightweight and absorbs well, making it a popular choice for massage oils and cosmetics.
6. **Sesame Oil (Sesamum indicum)**
   a. **Source:** Derived from sesame seeds.
   b. **Description:** Sesame oil is rich and slightly thicker, often used in traditional massage practices, including Ayurvedic treatments.
7. **Sunflower Oil (Helianthus annuus)**
   a. **Source:** Extracted from sunflower seeds.
   b. **Description:** Sunflower oil is light and non-greasy, often used as a base for lotions and creams.
8. **Avocado Oil (Persea americana)**
   a. **Source:** Derived from the flesh of avocados.

b. **Description:** A thick and deeply nourishing oil, avocado oil is rich in vitamins A, D, and E. It's great for dry or mature skin.

9. **Argan Oil (Argania spinosa)**
   a. **Source:** Extracted from the kernels of the argan tree.
   b. **Description:** Often called "liquid gold," argan oil is renowned for its moisturizing properties and is commonly used in haircare products.
10. **Castor Oil (Ricinus communis)**
   a. **Source:** Derived from castor beans.
   b. **Description:** Castor oil is thick and viscous, often used in haircare for its moisturizing properties and in traditional medicine as a laxative.

Waxes:

1. **Carnauba Wax (Copernicia prunifera)**
   a. **Source:** Extracted from the leaves of the Brazilian palm tree.
   b. **Description:** Known as the "queen of waxes," carnauba wax is hard, brittle, water-insoluble, and has a high melting point. It's used in cosmetic formulations, especially lipsticks, and also in car waxes, food products, and many other industrial applications.
2. **Candelilla Wax (Euphorbia antisyphilitica)**
   a. **Source:** Derived from the stems of the Candelilla shrub native to Mexico.
   b. **Description:** A vegan alternative to beeswax, this wax is rich, dense, and often used in lip balms, lotions, and cosmetic formulations.
3. **Beeswax (Apis mellifera)**
   a. **Source:** Produced by honey bees to construct their honeycombs.
   b. **Description:** Yellowish in color, beeswax is used in a variety of applications from candles to cosmetics, including creams, lotions, and lip

balms. It provides a protective barrier on the skin and offers anti-inflammatory properties.

4. **Jojoba Wax (Simmondsia chinensis)**
   a. **Source:** Derived from the seed oil of the jojoba plant. Even though it's often referred to as jojoba oil, it's technically a wax.
   b. **Description:** Unlike most waxes, jojoba is liquid at room temperature. It's very stable, doesn't oxidize easily, and closely resembles the skin's natural sebum.

Gums:

1. **Acacia Gum (Acacia senegal)**
   a. **Source:** Harvested from the sap of the Acacia tree.
   b. **Description**: Also known as gum arabic, this gum is edible and is often used in the food industry as a stabilizer. It also has applications in printmaking and cosmetics.
2. **Guar Gum (Cyamopsis tetragonoloba)**
   a. **Source**: Derived from guar beans.
   b. **Description:** It's a polysaccharide that is water-soluble. Widely used as a thickening and stabilizing agent in the food and cosmetic industries.
3. **Xanthan Gum**
   a. **Source:** Produced by fermenting sugars using the bacteria Xanthomonas campestris.
   b. **Description:** Often used in food and cosmetics as a thickening agent and stabilizer. It has an excellent ability to increase the viscosity of liquids.
4. **Tragacanth Gum (Astragalus gummifer)**
   a. **Source:** Obtained from the sap of the Astragalus shrub.

b. **Description**: Used in various applications, including food, cosmetics, and traditional medicine. It acts as a thickening agent and emulsifier.

5. **Chicle**
   a. **Source:** Harvested from the sap of the Sapodilla tree.
   b. **Description:** The traditional base for chewing gum before synthetic materials became predominant.

Colors:

1. **Henna (Lawsonia inermis)**
   a. **Source:** Leaves of the henna plant.
   b. **Description**: Yields a reddish-brown dye traditionally used for body art, hair coloring, and fabric dyeing in various cultures.
2. **Indigo (Indigofera tinctoria)**
   a. **Source:** Leaves of the indigo plant.
   b. **Description:** Produces a deep blue dye, historically significant in textile industries worldwide.
3. **Beetroot (Beta vulgaris)**
   a. **Source:** Root of the beet plant.
   b. **Description:** Provides a reddish to deep purple color, used in food products and cosmetics.
4. **Annatto (Bixa orellana)**
   a. **Source:** Seeds of the achiote tree.
   b. **Description:** Produces a yellow to reddish-orange colorant used in food products, textiles, and cosmetics.
5. **Saffron (Crocus sativus)**
   a. **Source:** Stigmas of the saffron crocus flower.

b. **Description:** Imparts a yellow-orange hue and is used in cooking, cosmetics, and historically in medicinal applications.

Perfumes:

1. **Rose (Rosa species)**
   a. **Source:** Petals of various rose species.
   b. **Description:** Yields a deeply floral and iconic scent. Rose essential oil and rosewater have been used for centuries in perfumes and cosmetics.
2. **Lavender (Lavandula angustifolia)**
   a. **Source:** Flowers of the lavender plant.
   b. **Description:** Lavender essential oil is renowned for its calming and therapeutic aroma, used extensively in perfumery and aromatherapy.
3. **Sandalwood (Santalum album)**
   a. **Source:** Heartwood of the sandalwood tree.
   b. **Description:** Sandalwood essential oil has a warm, woody, and rich scent, often used as a base note in perfumes.
4. **Jasmine (Jasminum species)**
   a. **Source:** Flowers of the jasmine plant.
   b. **Description:** Jasmine's intensely floral and exotic scent is a favorite in many high-end perfumes.
5. **Patchouli (Pogostemon cablin)**
   a. **Source:** Leaves of the patchouli plant.
   b. **Description:** Patchouli essential oil provides an earthy, musky aroma, and is frequently used as a base note in perfumes.
6. **Ylang-ylang (Cananga odorata)**
   a. **Source:** Flowers of the ylang-ylang tree.

b. **Description:** Ylang-ylang essential oil is prized for its sweet, floral, and slightly fruity aroma. It's a prominent component in various fragrances.

7. **Vetiver (Vetiveria zizanioides)**
   a. **Source:** Roots of the vetiver plant.
   b. **Description:** Vetiver oil has a complex woody, smoky, and earthy aroma. It's a common base note in many men's fragrances.

Protective Agents:

Protective agents, in this context, refer to materials that offer a shield or barrier, either physically or chemically, to prevent damage or deterioration.

1. **Aloe Vera (Aloe barbadensis miller)**
   a. **Source:** Gel from the leaves of the aloe vera plant.
   b. **Description:** Aloe vera is known for its soothing and healing properties. It provides a protective layer on the skin, which can help retain moisture and shield from environmental elements.
2. **Shea Butter (Vitellaria paradoxa)**
   a. **Source:** Fat extracted from the nuts of the shea tree.
   b. **Description:** Shea butter acts as an emollient, forming a protective barrier on the skin to prevent moisture loss and protect against environmental damage.
3. **Calendula (Calendula officinalis)**
   a. **Source:** Flowers of the calendula plant.
   b. **Description:** Calendula has been used traditionally to heal wounds and soothe skin. It offers a protective quality against skin irritations.
4. **Green Tea (Camellia sinensis)**
   a. **Source:** Leaves of the tea plant.

b. **Description:** Green tea is rich in antioxidants, especially epigallocatechin gallate (EGCG), which protect cells from damage by harmful free radicals.

Bleaching Agents:

Bleaching agents derived from plants are substances that can lighten or whiten a substrate, such as skin, hair, or fabric.

1. **Lemon Juice (Citrus limon)**
    a. **Source:** Juice from the lemon fruit.
    b. **Description:** The citric acid in lemon juice acts as a natural bleaching agent, often used to lighten hair and skin. However, it can be irritating and photosensitizing, so caution is advised.
2. **Licorice Root (Glycyrrhiza glabra)**
    a. **Source:** Extract from the root of the licorice plant.
    b. **Description:** Contains glabridin, which has been shown to inhibit melanin production, making it a natural skin-lightening agent.
3. **Turmeric (Curcuma longa)**
    a. **Source:** Rhizomes of the turmeric plant.
    b. **Description**: Turmeric has been reported to inhibit melanin production, potentially lightening skin, but it can temporarily stain the skin a yellowish color.
4. **Papaya (Carica papaya)**
    a. **Source:** Extract from papaya fruit.
    b. **Description:** Contains the enzyme papain, which can exfoliate dead skin cells and may have a mild bleaching effect
5. **Bearberry (Arctostaphylos uva-ursi)**
    a. **Source:** Extract from the bearberry plant.

b. **Description:** Contains arbutin, a compound that inhibits melanin production, making it a natural skin-lightening agent.

Multiple Choice Questions (Objective)

1. What is the Greek origin of the word 'cosmetics'?
   a. Kosmo
   b. Kostas
   c. Kosmeticos
   d. Kosmema
2. Which of the following is NOT a characteristic of herbal cosmetics?
   a. Eco-friendly
   b. Comprehensive range
   c. Synthetic additives
   d. Natural ingredients
3. Which herbal ingredient is known for its anti-acne properties?
   a. Saffron
   b. Neem
   c. Aloe Vera
   d. Lavender
4. Which oil is technically a liquid wax?
   a. Olive oil
   b. Coconut oil
   c. Jojoba oil
   d. Almond oil
5. Which wax is a vegan alternative to beeswax?
   a. Jojoba wax

b. Carnauba wax

c. Candelilla wax

d. Paraffin wax

6. What is the source of Xanthan Gum?

a. Harvested from the sap of the Sapodilla tree

b. Produced by fermenting sugars using the bacteria Xanthomonas campestris

c. Derived from guar beans

d. Obtained from the sap of the Astragalus shrub

7. Which colorant is used traditionally for body art?

a. Indigo

b. Henna

c. Annatto

d. Beetroot

8. Which perfume source yields a deeply floral and iconic scent?

a. Sandalwood

b. Jasmine

c. Patchouli

d. Rose

9. Which protective agent is known for its soothing and healing properties?

a. Green tea

b. Shea butter

c. Aloe vera

d. Calendula

10. What does the citric acid in lemon juice act as?

a. A protective agent

b. A bleaching agent

c. A thickening agent

d. A stabilizing agent

11. Herbal cosmetics are generally formulated using components derived from?

a. Synthetic chemicals

b. Minerals

c. Plants

d. Animal products

12. Which oil is known as "liquid gold"?

a. Argan oil

b. Sunflower oil

c. Grapeseed oil

d. Avocado oil

13. Which gum is the traditional base for chewing gum?

a. Xanthan gum

b. Guar gum

c. Chicle

d. Acacia gum

14. Which colorant produces a deep blue dye?

a. Henna

b. Beetroot

c. Indigo

d. Saffron

15. Which plant source provides a scent that is sweet, floral, and slightly fruity?

a. Lavender

b. Sandalwood

c. Vetiver

d. Ylang-ylang

16. Which of the following is not a source of a fixed oil?

a. Olive tree fruit

b. Coconut fruit meat

c. Jojoba plant seeds

d. Lemon fruit

17. Which of the following waxes is derived from a Brazilian palm tree?

a. Jojoba wax

b. Carnauba wax

c. Beeswax

d. Candelilla wax

18. What is the primary source of Guar gum?

a. Guar beans

b. Acacia tree sap

c. Sugars

d. Astragalus shrub sap

19. Which protective agent forms a barrier on the skin to prevent moisture loss?

a. Green tea

b. Aloe vera

c. Shea butter

d. Calendula

20. Which bleaching agent can exfoliate dead skin cells?

a. Lemon juice

b. Licorice root

c. Turmeric

d. Papaya

Short Answer Type Questions (Subjective)

1. Define herbal cosmetics.

2. Explain the origin of the word ‘cosmetics’.
3. List three therapeutic properties of herbal cosmetics.
4. Why might herbal cosmetics still pose allergic risks?
5. How do herbal cosmetics contribute to sustainability?
6. Describe the difference between fixed oils and essential oils.
7. How is olive oil beneficial in skincare formulations?
8. What makes jojoba oil unique among other fixed oils?
9. Explain the significance of carnauba wax in cosmetics.
10. How is xanthan gum produced and what is its primary use?
11. Describe the traditional use of henna.
12. How does the aroma of patchouli contribute to perfumes?
13. What is the primary role of protective agents in cosmetics?
14. Explain the bleaching properties of licorice root.
15. How can turmeric be both beneficial and problematic in skin care?
16. Describe the properties and uses of shea butter.
17. What are the potential benefits of using green tea in cosmetics?
18. How does lemon juice act as a natural bleaching agent?
19. Why is argan oil often referred to as "liquid gold"?
20. How does beeswax benefit the skin?

Long Answer Type Questions (Subjective)

1. Discuss the various advantages of using herbal cosmetics over traditional synthetic products.
2. Elaborate on the concerns and considerations that consumers should be aware of when choosing herbal cosmetics.
3. Describe the process of extraction and the benefits of using olive oil in cosmetic formulations.

4. Compare and contrast the properties and uses of carnauba wax, candelilla wax, and beeswax in cosmetics.
5. Explain the role of gums in cosmetic formulations and provide details on at least three different types of gums.
6. Describe the significance of using natural colorants in cosmetics and provide examples.
7. Discuss the importance and uses of perfumes derived from natural sources in aromatherapy and cosmetics.
8. Elaborate on the protective agents used in cosmetics and explain how they offer protection to the skin.
9. Discuss the concept and application of bleaching agents derived from plants in cosmetic formulations.
10. Highlight the difference between fixed oils and essential oils, providing examples and their significance in herbal cosmetics.

Answer Key of Multiple Choice Questions

1. (c) Kosmeticos
2. (c) Synthetic additives
3. (b) Neem
4. (c) Jojoba oil
5. (c) Candelilla wax
6. (b) Produced by fermenting sugars using the bacteria Xanthomonas campestris
7. (b) Henna
8. (d) Rose
9. (c) Aloe vera
10. (b) A bleaching agent
11. (c) Plants

12.(a) Argan oil

13.(c) Chicle

14.(c) Indigo

15.(d) Ylang-ylang

16.(d) Lemon fruit

17.(b) Carnauba wax

18.(a) Guar beans

19.(c) Shea butter

20.(d) Papaya

CHAPTER - 7

HERBAL EXCIPIENTS

Herbal excipients refer to natural substances derived from plant sources used in drug formulation to aid in the processes of manufacturing, compounding, dispensing, transporting, and storage. These excipients are not meant to exert therapeutic effects on their own but play vital roles in drug delivery and product stability. Here's an overview of some commonly used herbal excipients:

1. **Starches:** These are polysaccharides obtained from various plants such as maize (corn), rice, wheat, and potato. Starch is commonly used as a binder, filler, and Disintegrant in tablet formulation.
2. **Gums:** Natural gums like acacia gum, guar gum, and xanthan gum serve as binding and thickening agents in many formulations. They can also be used as matrix formers in controlled-release drug delivery systems.
3. **Cellulose derivatives:** These are semi-synthetic substances derived from natural cellulose. Examples include methylcellulose, hydroxyl propyl methylcellulose (HPMC), and carboxy methyl cellulose (CMC). They function as binders, thickeners, and controlled-release agents.
4. **Pectin:** Extracted from citrus fruits and apples, pectin is used in drug delivery systems as a gelling agent. It can also serve as a stabilizing and thickening agent in syrups.
5. **Agar:** Derived from certain seaweeds, agar functions as a gelling agent in pharmaceutical and cosmetic preparations.
6. **Alginates:** Obtained from brown seaweed, alginates can be employed as stabilizers, thickeners, and gelling agents in various formulations.
7. **Lecithin:** Extracted mainly from soybeans, lecithin acts as an emulsifier, helping to stabilize oil-in-water and water-in-oil emulsions.

8. **Aloe Vera Gel:** Extracted from the leaves of the aloe plant, this gel is often used in topical preparations for its soothing properties. It can also function as a base in various formulations.
9. **Oils and Fats:** Vegetable oils (e.g., sunflower oil, olive oil) and fats (e.g., cocoa butter) are often used as bases in ointments, creams, and suppositories.
10. **Essential Oils:** These are volatile compounds extracted from plants, often used to impart fragrance to a formulation and may also possess therapeutic properties. They may also serve as solvents or penetration enhancers in certain preparations.
11. **Tannins:** Found in various plants, tannins can act as astringents in topical applications.
12. **Saponins:** These are naturally occurring surfactants found in many plants. They can be used to enhance drug absorption and solubility.

HERBAL EXCIPIENTS – COLORANTS OF NATURAL ORIGIN

Colorants are agents that impart color to a formulation. In pharmaceuticals, they can make medications more identifiable and visually appealing, potentially improving patient compliance.

1. **Annatto (*Bixa orellana*)**
    a. **Source:** Seeds of the achiote tree.
    b. **Use & Significance:** Yields a yellow to orange color and is frequently used in food, cosmetics, and pharmaceuticals as a natural coloring agent.
2. **Beetroot Red (*Beta vulgaris*)**
    a. **Source:** Root of the beet plant.
    b. **Use & Significance:** Offers a pink to red hue and is popular in foods and lip products due to its natural origin and vibrant color.

3. **Chlorophyll (*Various Plants*)**
   a. **Source:** Green pigment in plants.
   b. **Use & Significance:** Provides a green color and is utilized in food and cosmetic products. It's also recognized for its deodorizing properties.
4. **Turmeric (*Curcuma longa*)**
   a. **Source:** Rhizomes of the turmeric plant.
   b. **Use & Significance:** Yields a yellow color and is widely used in foods. It's also an ingredient in some pharmaceutical and cosmetic products due to its anti-inflammatory properties in addition to its coloring capability.
5. **Saffron (*Crocus sativus*)**
   a. **Source:** Stigmas of the saffron crocus flower.
   b. **Use & Significance**: Gives a yellow-orange hue and is often used in culinary preparations. It has also found use as a natural colorant in certain cosmetics and pharmaceuticals.
6. **Indigo (*Indigofera tinctoria*)**
   a. **Source:** Leaves of the indigo plant.
   b. **Use & Significance:** Produces a blue dye and is traditionally significant in textiles. Its natural origin has led to its exploration as a colorant in various products.
7. **Henna (*Lawsonia inermis*)**
   a. **Source:** Leaves of the henna plant.
   b. **Use & Significance:** Offers a reddish-brown color and is popular for body art, hair coloring, and some cosmetic products.

Benefits of Using Natural Colorants:

1. **Consumer Appeal:** Many consumers now prefer products with natural ingredients due to perceived safety and holistic benefits.

2. **Potential Therapeutic Benefits:** Some natural colorants, like turmeric, also possess therapeutic properties, potentially adding value to the formulation.
3. **Environmentally Friendly:** Natural colorants are often seen as more eco-friendly than synthetic dyes, which may be derived from petroleum or other non-renewable sources.

Challenges:

1. **Consistency & Stability:** Natural colorants may show batch-to-batch variability, and some may fade or change color over time or under certain conditions.
2. **Cost:** Extraction and purification of natural colorants might be more expensive than producing synthetic ones.
3. **Potential Allergens:** Some individuals may be allergic or sensitive to natural ingredients.

The use of herbal excipients in pharmaceuticals and nutraceuticals continues to gain traction due to a growing demand for natural, organic, and eco-friendly products. Among the many roles that excipients can play, sweeteners and binders are two of the most prominent. Let's delve into the significance of natural substances as excipients, specifically focusing on sweeteners and binders:

HERBAL EXCIPIENTS – SWEETENERS OF NATURAL ORIGIN

Sweeteners are agents that impart a sweet taste to a formulation. They can mask the unpleasant taste of active ingredients and make oral formulations, such as syrups or chewable tablets, more palatable

1. **Stevia (*Stevia rebaudiana*)**
   a. **Source:** Leaves of the stevia plant.

b. **Use & Significance:** Steviol glycosides derived from stevia offer intense sweetness without calories, making stevia a popular choice for dietetic and diabetic formulations.

2. **Honey**
   a. **Source:** Bees processing flower nectar.
   b. **Use & Significance:** A natural sweetener with antimicrobial properties. It's used in traditional medicines, syrups, and throat lozenges.
3. **Agave Syrup**
   a. **Source:** Agave plant, primarily Agave tequilana.
   b. **Use & Significance:** natural sweet syrup often used as a sugar substitute in various preparations.
4. **Licorice (Glycyrrhiza glabra)**
   a. **Source**: Root of the licorice plant.
   b. **Use & Significance:** Contains glycyrrhizin, which is much sweeter than sugar and is often used in traditional medicines and candies.

HERBAL EXCIPIENTS – BINDERS OF NATURAL ORIGIN

Binders are substances used to hold the ingredients in a tablet together. They ensure the tablet remains intact after compression and give it strength.

1. **Gum Arabic (Acacia gum)**
   a. **Source:** Sap of the Acacia tree.
   b. **Use & Significance:** A natural binder, emulsifier, and thickening agent used in many pharmaceutical and food preparations.
2. **Tragacanth Gum**
   a. **Source:** Sap of the Astragalus species.

b. **Use & Significance:** Utilized as a binder and thickening agent in tablets and syrups.

3. **Guar Gum**

   a. **Source:** Seeds of the guar plant (*Cyamopsis tetragonoloba*).

   b. **Use & Significance:** Apart from its binding capabilities, guar gum can act as a thickener and stabilizer in various formulations.

4. **Xanthan Gum**

   a. **Source:** Produced by fermentation of glucose or sucrose by the bacterium *Xanthomonas campestris.*

   b. **Use & Significance:** Used as a binder, it also offers excellent viscosity and stabilizing properties, especially in syrups.

5. **Agar**

   a. **Source:** Derived from certain red algae or seaweeds.

   b. **Use & Significance:** In addition to binding, agar is commonly used as a gelling agent in pharmaceutical and cosmetic formulations.

Benefits of Using Natural Sweeteners and Binders:

1. **Consumer Appeal:** Natural origins often make products more appealing to health-conscious consumers.
2. **Holistic Benefits:** Some natural excipients, like honey, not only function as sweeteners but also offer therapeutic properties.
3. **Reduced Side Effects:** Natural excipients may have fewer side effects compared to their synthetic counterparts.

Challenges:

1. **Consistency & Stability:** Natural excipients can present variability from batch to batch and may be susceptible to microbial contamination.

2. **Cost:** Sourcing and processing natural excipients can be more expensive than synthetic ones.
3. **Limited Strength:** Some natural binders might not offer the same binding strength as synthetic ones, potentially affecting tablet durability.

Herbal excipients derived from natural substances play a crucial role in the design and formulation of pharmaceutical, nutraceutical, and cosmetic products. These naturally derived excipients can be especially appealing for those seeking greener or holistic alternatives. Let's explore the significance of natural substances used as diluents and viscosity builders:

HERBAL EXCIPIENTS – DILUENTS OF NATURAL ORIGIN

Diluents often referred to as fillers or bulking agents, are used to increase the bulk of a formulation, allowing for the production of a reasonably sized tablet or capsule when the dose of active ingredients is very small.

1. **Starches (e.g., Cornstarch, Rice Starch)**
   a. **Source:** Various plants such as maize (corn), rice, and potato.
   b. **Use & Significance:** A widely used natural diluent in tablet and capsule formulations. Starches can also act as Disintegrants, helping the tablet or capsule to break up in the digestive tract.
2. **Lactose**
   a. **Source:** Milk.
   b. **Use & Significance:** While of animal origin, lactose is a natural diluent used in many oral formulations. However, it's not suitable for lactose-intolerant individuals.
3. **Microcrystalline Cellulose**
   a. **Source:** Wood pulp.

b. **Use & Significance:** A semi-synthetic but naturally derived diluent that also serves as a binder and disintegrant in tablet formulations.

4. **Dicalcium Phosphate**
   a. **Source:** Mineral source.
   b. **Use & Significance:** Naturally derived and used as a diluent in tablet formulations.

HERBAL EXCIPIENTS – VISCOSITY BUILDERS OF NATURAL ORIGIN

Viscosity builders or thickeners increase the viscosity of a liquid formulation, improving its texture and ensuring uniform dispersion of active ingredients.

1. **Acacia Gum (Gum Arabic)**
   a. **Source:** Sap of the Acacia tree.
   b. **Use & Significance:** Acts as a natural thickener in syrups and other liquid preparations.
2. **Agar**
   a. **Source:** Certain red algae or seaweeds.
   b. **Use & Significance**: Used as a gelling agent and viscosity enhancer in pharmaceutical and cosmetic preparations.
3. **Guar Gum**
   a. **Source:** Seeds of the guar plant (*Cyamopsis tetragonoloba*).
   b. **Use & Significance:** A polysaccharide that acts as a viscosity builder in various formulations.
4. **Xanthan Gum**
   a. **Source:** Produced by fermentation of glucose or sucrose by the bacterium *Xanthomonas campestris.*
   b. **Use & Significance**: Widely used for its thickening and stabilizing properties in various liquid formulations.

5. **Alginate**
    a. **Source:** Extracted from brown seaweeds.
    b. **Use & Significance:** Alginates can be used to enhance the viscosity of a formulation and are also known for their gelling properties.

Benefits of Using Natural Diluents and Viscosity Builders:

1. **Perceived Safety:** Many consumers view naturally derived excipients as safer than synthetic alternatives.
2. **Compatibility:** Natural excipients can offer better compatibility with other natural ingredients in a formulation.
3. Eco-friendliness: Natural excipients are often more sustainable and eco-friendly.

Challenges

1. **Consistency:** Natural excipients may exhibit batch-to-batch variability.
2. **Stability:** Some natural excipients might be more susceptible to microbial growth or degradation over time.
3. **Cost:** The processing of natural excipients can sometimes be more expensive than their synthetic counterparts.

Excipients are integral components in pharmaceutical formulations, as they help improve the drug's properties, stability, and overall patient compliance. With the growing interest in natural and holistic products, herbal excipients derived from natural substances have become increasingly popular. Here, we'll delve into the significance of substances of natural origin used as Disintegrants, flavours, and perfumes:

HERBAL EXCIPIENTS – DISINTEGRANTS OF NATURAL ORIGIN

Disintegrants ensure that when a tablet comes into contact with a liquid, it breaks apart into smaller particles, making the active ingredient available for absorption.

1. **Starches (e.g., Cornstarch, Potato Starch)**
    a. **Source:** Various plants such as maize (corn) and potato.
    b. **Use & Significance**: Starches have been traditionally used as disintegrants, helping tablets to rapidly break apart in the digestive tract.
2. **Alginates**
    a. **Source:** Extracted from brown seaweeds.
    b. **Use & Significance:** Alginates can absorb water quickly, aiding in the disintegration process of tablets.
3. **Plant fibers (e.g., Psyllium husk)**
    a. **Source:** Seeds of the Plantago ovata plant.
    b. **Use & Significance:** Psyllium husk can swell upon contact with water, aiding in the disintegration of tablets.

HERBAL EXCIPIENTS – FLAVORS OF NATURAL ORIGIN

Flavors are added to mask the unpleasant taste of active ingredients, making oral formulations more palatable, especially for pediatric and geriatric patients.

1. **Menthol**
    a. **Source:** Extracted from peppermint or mint oils.
    b. **Use & Significance:** Provides a cooling sensation and pleasant taste, commonly used in cough and cold formulations.
2. **Ginger extract**
    a. **Source:** Ginger root.
    b. **Use & Significance:** Used to mask taste and also has therapeutic properties.

3. **Fennel oil**
    a. **Source:** Fennel seeds.
    b. **Use & Significance**: Provides a pleasant taste and aroma, often used in digestive preparations.

HERBAL EXCIPIENTS – PERFUMES OF NATURAL ORIGI

Perfumes or fragrances are typically used in topical preparations to provide a pleasant smell or mask any undesirable odors.

1. **Lavender oil**
    a. **Source:** Lavender plant.
    b. **Use & Significance:** Known for its calming scent, it's commonly used in topical preparations and aromatherapy.
2. **Eucalyptus oil**
    a. **Source:** Eucalyptus tree.
    b. **Use & Significance:** Has a distinct aroma and is also recognized for its antimicrobial properties.
3. **Rose oil**
    a. **Source:** Rose petals.
    b. **Use & Significance:** Provides a luxurious and calming scent, often used in high-end cosmetics and skincare.

Benefits of Using Natural Disintegrants, Flavors, and Perfumes:

1. **Patient Compliance:** Natural flavors can make medications more palatable, leading to increased patient compliance.
2. **Perceived Safety:** Consumers often perceive natural ingredients as safer and more wholesome.

3. **Multifunctionality:** Some natural excipients, like ginger, can serve both as flavoring agents and possess therapeutic properties.

Challenges:

1. **Consistency:** Natural sources can have batch-to-batch variability.
2. **Stability:** Natural excipients might be more prone to degradation or may have shorter shelf lives.
3. **Potential Allergens:** Some natural flavors or perfumes can cause allergic reactions in sensitive individuals.

In summary, while herbal excipients offer a range of benefits, it's essential to choose them carefully, considering their properties, stability, and potential interactions with other ingredients in a formulation.

Multiple Choice Questions (MCQs)

1. Which of the following is NOT a source of starch used as an herbal excipient?

   a) Maize (corn)

   b) Rice

   c) Soybean

   d) Potato

2. Which natural gum can also be used as a matrix former in controlled-release drug delivery systems?

   a) Acacia gum

   b) Xanthan gum

   c) Guar gum

   d) Tragacanth Gum

3. Which cellulose derivative functions as binders, thickeners, and controlled-release agents?

   a) Hydroxypropyl methylcellulose (HPMC)

b) Starch

c) Pectin

d) Guar gum

4. Which natural substance is used as a gelling agent in drug delivery systems?

   a) Lecithin

   b) Alginate

   c) Agar

   d) Aloe Vera Gel

5. Which of the following is NOT a natural colorant?

   a) Beetroot Red

   b) Chlorophyll

   c) Tartrazine

   d) Henna

6. Which of the following sweeteners is calorie-free?

   a) Stevia

   b) Honey

   c) Agave Syrup

   d) Sugar

7. Which binder is derived from the sap of the Acacia tree?

   a) Guar Gum

   b) Xanthan Gum

   c) Gum Arabic

   d) Agar

8. Which viscosity builder is derived from certain red algae or seaweeds?

   a) Alginate

   b) Xanthan Gum

   c) Acacia Gum

d) Agar

9. Which of the following Disintegrant swells upon contact with water?
   a) Starches
   b) Alginates
   c) Plant fibers (e.g., Psyllium husk)
   d) Microcrystalline Cellulose
10. Which flavoring agent provides a cooling sensation and is commonly used in cough and cold formulations?
   a) Ginger extract
   b) Fennel oil
   c) Menthol
   d) Rose oil
11. The scent of which perfume is known for its calming properties?
   a) Lavender oil
   b) Eucalyptus oil
   c) Rose oil
   d) Lemon oil
12. Which herbal excipient is recognized for its antimicrobial properties and distinct aroma?
   a) Rose oil
   b) Lavender oil
   c) Eucalyptus oil
   d) Jasmine oil
13. What is the primary role of disintegrants in tablet formulation?
   a) Add flavor
   b) Provide a pleasant smell
   c) Increase tablet size

d) Ensure tablets break apart in the digestive tract

14. Which natural substance is used to mask the taste of active ingredients and also has therapeutic properties?

a) Menthol

b) Ginger extract

c) Eucalyptus oil

d) Fennel oil

15. Which of the following herbal excipients is NOT a viscosity builder?

a) Agar

b) Xanthan Gum

c) Lecithin

d) Alginate

16. Derived from the leaves of the stevia plant, which sweetener offers intense sweetness without calories?

a) Honey

b) Agave Syrup

c) Stevia

d) Sugar

17. Which of the following is a natural source of the diluent used in tablet and capsule formulations?

a) Wood pulp

b) Seaweeds

c) Maize (corn)

d) Milk

18. Which of the following is NOT a natural perfume used in topical preparations?

a) Lavender oil

b) Eucalyptus oil

c) Menthol

d) Rose oil

19. What is the primary function of diluents in drug formulations?

a) Act as a fragrance

b) Increase the bulk of a formulation

c) Act as a thickener

d) Provide a cooling sensation

20. Which herbal excipient is recognized for its deodorizing properties?

a) Henna

b) Turmeric

c) Chlorophyll

d) Annatto

Short Answer Type Questions (Subjective)

1. Define herbal excipients and their significance in drug formulation.
2. List three sources of starch used in herbal excipients.
3. How is pectin used in drug delivery systems?
4. What is the significance of lecithin in drug formulations?
5. Explain the role of tannins as herbal excipients.
6. How is the annatto used as a colorant of natural origin?
7. What are the benefits of using honey as a natural sweetener?
8. Describe the use and significance of gum Arabic in pharmaceutical formulations.
9. How do natural colorants benefit pharmaceutical products?
10. List three challenges associated with using natural diluents and viscosity builders.
11. Describe the role of alginates as disintegrants.

12. Explain the significance of ginger extract as a flavoring agent.
13. How is rose oil used as a perfume in pharmaceutical preparations?
14. What is the role of diluents in pharmaceutical formulations?
15. How do starches function as disintegrants in tablet formulations?
16. Describe the significance of menthol as a flavoring agent.
17. Explain the benefits of using natural disintegrants, flavors, and perfumes.
18. List three sources of natural diluents.
19. Describe the significance of lavender oil as a natural perfume.
20. How is chlorophyll used as a natural colorant?

Long Answer Type Questions (Subjective)

1. Discuss the various roles of herbal excipients in pharmaceutical formulations, highlighting their significance and benefits.
2. Compare and contrast the properties and uses of different natural colorants in pharmaceutical formulations.
3. Describe the advantages and challenges associated with using natural sweeteners and binders in drug formulations.
4. Elaborate on the various natural sources of diluents and explain their significance in pharmaceutical preparations.
5. Discuss the importance and applications of natural viscosity builders in drug formulations.
6. Describe the role and significance of natural disintegrants in tablet formulations, providing examples.
7. Explain the importance of flavors in pharmaceutical formulations and highlight some natural sources used.
8. Discuss the significance of natural perfumes in pharmaceutical and cosmetic formulations, elaborating on their sources and benefits.

9. Describe the challenges associated with using herbal excipients in drug formulations and discuss potential solutions.
10. Highlight the multifunctional roles of certain herbal excipients, providing examples and their significance.

Answer Key of Multiple-Choice Questions:

1. (c) Soybean
2. (a) Acacia gum
3. (a) Hydroxypropyl methylcellulose (HPMC)
4. (c) Agar
5. (c) Tartrazine
6. (a) Stevia
7. (c) Gum Arabic
8. (d) Agar
9. (c) Plant fibers (e.g., Psyllium husk)
10. (c) Menthol
11. (a) Lavender oil
12. (c) Eucalyptus oil
13. (d) Ensure tablets break apart in the digestive tract
14. (b) Ginger extract
15. (c) Lecithin
16. (c) Stevia
17. (c) Maize (corn)
18. (c) Menthol
19. (b) Increase the bulk of a formulation
20. (c) Chlorophyll

CHAPTER - 8

HERBAL FORMULATIONS

Herbal formulations have been used for thousands of years in traditional systems of medicine around the world. They can be in the form of teas, tinctures, powders, capsules, ointments, and more. Below are some examples of popular herbal formulations from various traditions:

1. **Ayurveda (Traditional Indian Medicine):**
   a. **Triphala:** A combination of three fruits - Amalaki (Emblica officinalis), Bibhitaki (Terminalia bellirica), and Haritaki (Terminalia chebula). It is often used for digestion and detoxification.
   b. **Chyawanprash:** A jam-like mixture made from various herbs and honey. Primarily contains Amla (Indian gooseberry) and is considered a rejuvenating tonic.
2. **Traditional Chinese Medicine (TCM):**
   a. **Yin Qiao San:** Used to treat the early stages of colds or flu.
   b. **Liu Wei Di Huang Wan:** Commonly used for kidney and liver yin deficiency.
3. **Western Herbalism:**
   a. **Echinacea tincture:** Used to stimulate the immune system.
   b. **Valerian root:** Often used as a sedative and for insomnia.
4. **Traditional African Medicine**:
   a. **African potato:** Used for a range of conditions, including urinary tract infections and immune boosting.
   b. **Rooibos tea:** A popular antioxidant-rich tea from South Africa.
5. **Amazonian Traditional Medicine:**

a. **Pau d'arco:** Bark from a tree used traditionally for various infections.

b. **Cat's Claw (Una de Gato):** Believed to be anti-inflammatory and immune-boosting.

6. **European Traditional Medicine:**

   a. **St. John's Wort:** Commonly used for mild to moderate depression.

   b. **Chamomile tea:** Often consumed for relaxation and to aid sleep.

GUIDELINES FOR USING HERBAL FORMULATIONS:

1. **Consult a healthcare professional**: Before starting any herbal remedies, it's essential to consult with a healthcare professional, especially if you're already on medications. Some herbs can interact with medicines.
2. **Quality Matters:** Purchase herbal products from reputable sources to ensure quality, potency, and safety. Some products can be adulterated or contaminated.
3. **Allergies & Side Effects:** Even if it's natural, it doesn't mean it's always safe for everyone. Be aware of any allergies you might have, and be cautious of potential side effects.
4. **Pregnancy & Breastfeeding:** Many herbal formulations are not recommended during pregnancy and breastfeeding. Always consult with a healthcare provider.

HERBAL SYRUPS

Definition: Syrups are thick, viscous liquid dosage forms that contain a high concentration of sucrose or other sugars. Herbal syrups are prepared by dissolving sugar in an aqueous infusion or decoction of medicinal herbs, sometimes with the addition of preservatives, flavors, or colors. The sugar acts as both a sweetener and a preservative.

Herbal syrups are a common and pleasant way to administer medicinal herbs, especially for those who might find alcohol tinctures or teas unpalatable. The basic idea is to create a concentrated decoction or infusion of the herb(s), and then preserve and sweeten this with sugar or honey to make a syrup. The sugar and honey also contribute their own therapeutic properties.

Here are some conventional herbal syrup formulations:

1. **Elderberry Syrup:** Elderberries (Sambucus nigra) are renowned for their immune-boosting properties, especially in fighting colds and flu.
2. **Ginger Syrup:** Made from fresh ginger root, this syrup is warming and can help with digestion, nausea, and cold symptoms.
3. **Thyme Syrup:** Thyme is antiseptic and antispasmodic. It's beneficial for respiratory issues, coughs, and bronchitis.
4. **Mullein and Garlic Ear Oil Syrup:** A combination that's often used for ear infections. While garlic has antibiotic properties, mullein can be soothing.
5. **Marshmallow Root Syrup:** Marshmallow root is demulcent, making it soothing for irritated mucous membranes, such as a sore throat or irritated digestive tract.
6. **Horehound Syrup:** Horehound (Marrubium vulgare) is a traditional remedy for coughs and congestion.
7. **Cherry Bark Syrup:** Wild cherry bark is antitussive, helping calm a persistent cough.
8. **Licorice Root Syrup:** Licorice is an adaptogen and can be soothing for the throat and beneficial for the adrenal glands.

Basic Method to Prepare Herbal Syrup:

1. **Decoction/Infusion:** Start by making a strong decoction (for harder plant materials like roots or bark) or infusion (for leaves or flowers) with the herb.

This involves simmering or steeping the herbs in water to extract their medicinal constituents.

2. **Straining:** Once the decoction or infusion is ready, strain out the plant material using a fine strainer or cheesecloth.
3. **Adding Sweetener:** While the liquid is still warm, add your sweetener. Typically, for every cup of liquid, you'll add approximately 1 cup of sugar or honey, but this can be adjusted based on your taste and desired consistency.
4. **Bottling:** Once your sweetener is thoroughly dissolved, transfer your syrup to a clean glass bottle.
5. **Preservation:** If you'd like to extend the shelf life of your syrup, you can add a small amount of brandy or vodka as a preservative.

Store the finished syrup in the refrigerator. Generally, herbal syrups last anywhere from a few weeks to several months when stored correctly, depending on the ingredients and any preservatives used.

Note: Always consult with a healthcare professional before using any herbal formulation to ensure it is safe for you, especially if you are pregnant, breastfeeding, or on medications.

Elderberry Syrup Formulation:

1. **Primary Constituent:**
   a. **Elderberries (*Sambucus nigra*):** Elderberries are the star ingredient in this syrup. They have been traditionally used for their antiviral properties, especially against the flu and common cold. They are rich in vitamins (especially vitamin C), minerals, and antioxidants.
2. **Secondary Constituents (these can vary based on the formulation and the desired effect):**

a. **Ginger (*Zingiber officinale*):** Warming and helpful for improving circulation. It's also good for its anti-nausea and anti-inflammatory properties.
b. **Cinnamon (*Cinnamomum verum*):** Warming and can help improve circulation and digestion. Also, it's flavorful and aromatic.
c. **Cloves (Syzygium aromaticum):** Can provide pain relief and have antiseptic properties. They add a warming and aromatic flavor.

3. **Solvent:**
   a. **Water:** Used to extract the constituents from the herbs in the form of a decoction.
4. **Sweetener/Preservative:**
   a. **Raw Honey:** Acts as both a sweetener and a mild preservative. Honey also brings its own medicinal qualities, being anti-inflammatory and soothing for sore throats.
   b. **Optional:** A splash of brandy or vodka can be added as a stronger preservative to prolong shelf life.

Method:

1. Combine elderberries with water in a pot and bring to a boil. You can also add ginger, cinnamon, and cloves.
2. Reduce heat and simmer until the liquid has reduced by about half. This usually takes 45 minutes to an hour.
3. Remove from heat and mash the berries to release any remaining juice.

5. Strain the mixture through a fine strainer or cheesecloth to remove solid constituents.
6. While the liquid is still warm (but not boiling hot), add honey. Stir until fully

dissolved.

7. If using, add the splash of brandy or vodka for preservation.
8. Once cooled, transfer the syrup to a clean glass bottle.

This syrup can be consumed directly, usually in doses of a tablespoon for adults or a teaspoon for children (though always consult with a healthcare professional). It can be taken as a preventative measure during flu season or at the first sign of illness.

Examples:

1. **Bronchial Soothing Syrup:**
    a. **Purpose:** To soothe coughs and support bronchial health.
    b. **Herbal Constituents:** Mullein (Verbascum thapsus), marshmallow root (Althaea officinalis), and licorice root (Glycyrrhiza glabra).
    c. **Additional Components:** Honey or sugar (as a sweetener and preservative), water, and sometimes a bit of brandy or other alcohol as a preservative.
2. **Elderberry Syrup:**
    a. **Purpose:** Immune support, especially during the cold and flu season.
    b. **Herbal Constituent:** Elderberries (Sambucus nigra).
    c. **Additional Components:** Sugar or honey, water, and optional additions like cinnamon or ginger for flavor and extra benefits.
3. **Soothing Throat Syrup:**
    a. **Purpose:** Relief from sore throats and related discomfort.
    b. **Herbal Constituents:** Slippery elm bark (Ulmus rubra), wild cherry bark (Prunus serotina), and echinacea (Echinacea spp.).
    c. **Additional Components:** Honey or sugar, water, and possibly lemon for flavor and vitamin C.
4. **Relaxation Syrup:**

a. **Purpose:** To promote relaxation and ease tension.
b. **Herbal Constituents:** Lemon balm (Melissa officinalis), chamomile (Matricaria recutita), and passionflower (Passiflora incarnata).
c. **Additional Components:** Honey or sugar and water.

To make basic herbal syrup:

1. Prepare a strong decoction or infusion of the chosen herb(s).
2. Strain the liquid and, while still warm, add an equal volume of sugar or honey, stirring until it's completely dissolved.
3. Once cooled, you can transfer the syrup to a sterilized bottle for storage. Some people also add a small amount of alcohol or citric acid as a preservative.

Herbal syrups are a favorite for those who prefer a sweet-tasting, easy-to-consume format, especially for children. However, always consult a healthcare professional or qualified herbalist before administering any herbal remedies.

MIXTURES

"Mixtures" in pharmaceutical terms typically refer to liquid preparations that contain one or more soluble chemical substances dissolved in a suitable solvent or mixture of mutually miscible solvents. Herbal mixtures, in this context, will be liquid preparations containing one or more herbal constituents. Here are some examples:

1. **Cough Mixture:**
   a. **Primary Constituents:** Licorice root extract (soothing and anti-inflammatory), horehound extract (useful for coughs and bronchitis), and marshmallow root extract (soothing and mucilaginous).
   b. **Solvent:** Glycerin or alcohol for extraction and as a base.

   c. **Flavoring Agents:** Honey or sugar for sweetness, and perhaps a small amount of essential oils like peppermint or eucalyptus for flavor and their own therapeutic benefits.

2. **Digestive Mixture:**
   a. **Primary Constituents:** Peppermint leaf extract (antispasmodic and digestive aid), fennel seed extract (helpful for bloating and gas), and ginger root extract (anti-nausea and promotes digestion).
   b. **Solvent:** Alcohol or water.
   c. **Flavoring Agents:** Anise or caraway for a pleasant taste and additional digestive support.
3. **Relaxing Sleep Mixture:**
   a. **Primary Constituents:** Valerian root extract (a natural sedative), passionflower extract (calms restlessness), and lemon balm extract (reduces anxiety and induces calm).
   b. **Solvent:** Alcohol, as many of these herbs extract better in alcohol.
   c. **Flavoring Agents:** Honey or sugar for sweetness, with possible chamomile for flavor and additional calming effects.
4. **Liver Support Mixture:**
   a. **Primary Constituents:** Milk thistle seed extract (a renowned liver support herb), dandelion root extract (supports bile flow), and turmeric root extract (anti-inflammatory and liver protective).
   b. **Solvent:** Alcohol for effective extraction.
   c. **Flavoring Agents:** Honey or sugar for taste.

Method of Preparation:

1. Start with the solvent (like water or alcohol) and the herbs in their respective ratios.

2. For alcohol-based tinctures, the herbs are typically macerated (soaked) in the solvent for a few weeks, then strained out. For water-based mixtures or decoctions, the herbs are typically boiled in water and then reduced to the desired concentration.
3. After straining, while the liquid is still warm, flavoring agents like honey or sugar can be added.
4. Once the mixture has cooled and been thoroughly mixed, it can be bottled in clean, sterile containers.

Always label the bottles with the date of preparation and the contents, as well as any instructions for use.

Note: The above mixtures are generic examples and may not be suitable for everyone. It's crucial to consult a healthcare professional or qualified herbalist before starting any herbal regimen.

Conventional herbal mixtures

"Conventional herbal mixtures" typically refers to combinations of herbs blended together in specific ratios to create a therapeutic effect. These mixtures can come in various forms such as teas, tinctures, or powdered blends. Here are some classic examples:

1. Tonic Tea Mixture:

a. Purpose: General health and vitality.
b. Herbs Used:
c. Nettle leaves (Urtica dioica) - Nutritive and supports blood health.
d. Red clover blossoms (Trifolium pratense) - Detoxifying and hormone-balancing.
e. Dandelion root (Taraxacum officinale) - Liver support.

f. Form: Dried herbs mixed together and steeped as a tea.

2. **Calm and Relax Mixture:**
    a. Purpose: To help reduce stress and promote relaxation.
    b. Herbs Used:
    c. Chamomile flowers (Matricaria recutita) - Calming and soothing.
    d. Lavender buds (Lavandula angustifolia) - Reduces anxiety.
    e. Lemon balm leaves (Melissa officinalis) - Relieves nervous tension.
    f. Form: Dried herbs mixed and steeped as a tea or blended as a tincture.
3. **Immune Boosting Tincture Mixture:**
    a. Purpose: Support and strengthen the immune system.
    b. Herbs Used:
    c. Echinacea root (*Echinacea purpurea*) - Immune modulating.
    d. Astragalus root (*Astragalus membranaceus*) - Deep immune system tonic.
    e. Elderberries (*Sambucus nigra*) - Antiviral and immune-supportive.
    f. Form: Herbs macerated in alcohol to create a tincture.
4. **Digestive Powder Mixture:**
    a. Purpose: Improve digestion and reduce bloating.
    b. Herbs Used:
    c. Fennel seeds (*Foeniculum vulgare*) - Carminative, reduces gas.
    d. Peppermint leaves (Mentha piperita) - Eases digestive spasms.
    e. Slippery elm bark (Ulmus rubra) - Soothing and mucilaginous.
    f. Form: Ground herbs mixed into a fine powder and taken with water or sprinkled on food.
5. **Detox and Cleanse Mixture:**
    a. Purpose: Detoxification and cleansing.
    b. Herbs Used:
    c. Milk thistle seeds (*Silybum marianum*) - Liver protective and restorative.

d. Burdock root (*Arctium lappa*) - Blood purifying.
e. Cleavers (*Galium aparine*) - Lymphatic cleanser.
f. Form: Dried herbs used to prepare a decoction or as a tincture.

Note: Formulations and their indications may vary based on traditional usage, local practices, and the knowledge base of the herbalist. It's important to consult with a knowledgeable herbal practitioner or a healthcare professional before taking any herbal preparations.

CONVENTIONAL HERBAL FORMULATIONS: TABLETS

Definition: Tablets are solid dosage forms that typically comprise a medicinal substance in combination with excipients such as binders, fillers, disintegrants, and coatings. They're widely used due to their stability, ease of transport, and convenience for the end user.

Tablets are solid dosage forms that are prepared by compressing a single dose of medicinal agents. They are the most widely used dosage form due to their convenience.

1. **Turmeric Tablets:**
    a. **Purpose:** Anti-inflammatory, antioxidant.
    b. **Active Constituent:** Curcumin from turmeric root (Curcuma longa).
    c. **Excipients:** Binders, fillers, and coatings for stability and ease of consumption.
2. **Ginkgo Biloba Tablets:**
    a. **Purpose:** Improve memory and cognitive function.
    b. **Active Constituent:** Flavonoids and terpenoids from Ginkgo leaves.
    c. **Excipients:** Binders, fillers, and coatings.
3. **Milk Thistle Tablets:**

a. **Purpose:** Liver support and detoxification.
b. **Active Constituent:** Silymarin from milk thistle seeds (Silybum marianum).
c. **Excipients:** Binders, fillers, and coatings.

Examples:

1. **Ashwagandha Tablets:**
    a. **Purpose:** Adaptogen, stress relief, and general well-being.
    b. **Active Constituent:** Withanolides from Ashwagandha root (Withania somnifera).
    c. **Excipients**: Microcrystalline cellulose (filler and binder), magnesium stearate (lubricant), silicon dioxide (anti-caking agent).
2. **St. John's Wort Tablets:**
    a. **Purpose:** Mood support and mild antidepressant.
    b. **Active Constituent:** Hypericin from St. John's Wort herb (Hypericum perforatum).
    c. **Excipients:** Dicalcium phosphate (filler and binder), maltodextrin (filler), vegetable stearic acid (lubricant).

NOVEL DOSAGE FORMS: PHYTOSOMES

Definition: Phytosomes are a patented, advanced form of herbal product where the active component of the herb is bound to phospholipids, primarily phosphatidylcholine. This enhances the absorption and bioavailability of the herb. The idea is to make the herbal compounds more lipid-like,

Phytosomes are advanced forms of herbal products that are better absorbed and produce better results than conventional herbal extracts. They are complexed with phospholipids, which enhances their absorption.

1. **Green Tea Phytosome:**
   a. **Purpose:** Antioxidant, cardiovascular support.
   b. **Active Constituent:** Polyphenols from green tea (Camellia sinensis) complexed with phosphatidylcholine.
   c. **Benefits:** Improved absorption leading to enhanced antioxidant activity in the body.
2. **Milk Thistle Phytosome**:
   a. **Purpose:** Enhanced liver support.
   b. **Active Constituent:** Silymarin complexed with phospholipids.
   c. **Benefits:** Better liver protection due to improved bioavailability.
3. **Grape Seed Phytosome:**
   a. **Purpose:** Antioxidant and cardiovascular support.
   b. **Active Constituent**: Proanthocyanidins from grape seeds complexed with phospholipids.
   c. **Benefits**: Enhanced vascular health due to better absorption.

Benefits of Phytosomes:

1. **Improved Bioavailability:** The lipid-soluble character of the phospholipid complex makes it easier for the molecules to pass through the lipid-rich outer portion of the intestinal membrane into the cell, leading to better absorption of the active constituents.
2. **Stability:** Phytosomes are more stable than their non-complexed counterparts.
3. **Enhanced Clinical Efficacy:** Due to better absorption, often lower doses of phytosomes can achieve the same therapeutic effects as higher doses of the regular herbal extracts.

Thus improving their ability to be absorbed through the cell membrane.

Examples:

1. **Curcumin Phytosome:**
   a. **Purpose:** Anti-inflammatory, antioxidant.
   b. **Active Constituent:** Curcumin from turmeric root (Curcuma longa) complexed with phosphatidylcholine.
   c. **Benefits:** Traditional curcumin extracts are poorly absorbed in the gut. The phytosomal form enhances absorption, leading to a greater anti-inflammatory effect.
2. **Silybin Phytosome:**
   a. **Purpose:** Liver protection and detoxification.
   b. **Active Constituent**: Silybin, the most active component of silymarin from milk thistle seeds (Silybum marianum), complexed with phosphatidylcholine.
   c. **Benefits:** Silybin phytosome is better absorbed than conventional silymarin extracts, offering enhanced liver protection.
3. **Green Tea Phytosome:**
   a. **Purpose:** Antioxidant and weight management.
   b. **Active Constituent:** Polyphenols, especially epigallocatechin gallate (EGCG), from green tea (Camellia sinensis) leaves complexed with phosphatidylcholine.
   c. **Benefits:** Improved oral bioavailability leading to enhanced antioxidant activity and potentially better clinical outcomes for weight management.

Multiple Choice Questions (MCQs):

1. Which of the following is NOT a part of the Triphala formulation in Ayurveda?
   a. Amalaki
   b. Bibhitaki
   c. Neem

d. Haritaki

2. Which herbal formulation from Traditional Chinese Medicine (TCM) is used for kidney and liver yin deficiency?

   a. Liu Wei Di Huang Wan

   b. Yin Qiao San

   c. Triphala

   d. Chyawanprash

3. What is the primary purpose of Valerian root in Western Herbalism?

   a. Immune system boost

   b. Digestion aid

   c. Sedative and insomnia relief

   d. Detoxification

4. Which of these is NOT a form of herbal formulation?

   a. Syrup

   b. Tablet

   c. Phytosome

   d. Injection

5. What is the primary role of sugar in herbal syrups?

   a. Flavor enhancer

   b. Preservative

   c. Active ingredient

   d. Both a and b

6. Which herb is antiseptic and antispasmodic, beneficial for respiratory issues?

   a. Mullein

   b. Ginger

   c. Thyme

   d. Horehound

7. Elderberry Syrup primarily contains which vitamin?
   a. Vitamin A
   b. Vitamin C
   c. Vitamin D
   d. Vitamin E
8. What is the main component in Ashwagandha Tablets?
   a. Curcumin
   b. Hypericin
   c. Withanolides
   d. Silymarin
9. What is the primary advantage of phytosomes over traditional herbal extracts?
   a. Better taste
   b. Longer shelf life
   c. Improved bioavailability
   d. Lower cost
10. Which herbal formulation is used to improve memory and cognitive function?
   a. Turmeric Tablets
   b. Ginkgo Biloba Tablets
   c. Milk Thistle Tablets
   d. Ginger Syrup
11. Which herb in Ayurveda is considered a rejuvenating tonic?
   a. Triphala
   b. Chyawanprash
   c. Yin Qiao San
   d. Echinacea tincture
12. Rooibos tea, a popular antioxidant-rich tea, originates from which region?
   a. India

b. China

c. South Africa

d. Europe

13.Cat's Claw (Una de Gato) is believed to have which of the following properties?

a. Immune-boosting

b. Sedative

c. Digestive

d. Energizing

14.St. John's Wort is commonly used to treat what condition?

a. Insomnia

b. Mild to moderate depression

c. Digestion problems

d. Cold and flu

15.Which component in phytosomes makes herbal compounds more lipid-like?

a. Sugar

b. Alcohol

c. Phospholipids

d. Water

16.What is the primary constituent of Turmeric Tablets?

a. Silymarin

b. Withanolides

c. Curcumin

d. Hypericin

17.Licorice Root Syrup is beneficial for which part of the body?

a. Liver

b. Heart

c. Lungs

d. Adrenal glands

18. Which herb is renowned for immune-boosting properties, especially against colds and flu?

a. Ginger

b. Thyme

c. Elderberries

d. Licorice root

19. Which component is often added to herbal syrups to prolong their shelf life?

a. Sugar

b. Water

c. Brandy or vodka

d. Lemon juice

20. What is the primary purpose of Echinacea tincture in Western Herbalism?

a. Aid sleep

b. Stimulate the immune system

c. Promote relaxation

d. Improve digestion

Short Answer Type Questions (Subjective):

1. List the three fruits that make up the Triphala formulation in Ayurveda.
2. What is the primary ingredient in Chyawanprash?
3. Explain the use of Yin Qiao San in Traditional Chinese Medicine.
4. Describe the benefits of Valerian root in Western Herbalism.
5. What is the traditional use of the African potato in Traditional African Medicine?
6. Name two properties of Cat's Claw in Amazonian Traditional Medicine.

7. What are the primary uses of St. John's Wort in European Traditional Medicine?
8. Describe the role of sugar in herbal syrups.
9. List the primary and secondary constituents of the Elderberry Syrup formulation.
10. What is the method of preparation for the Elderberry Syrup formulation?
11. Explain the purpose of the Bronchial Soothing Syrup.
12. How is a herbal syrup different from a tincture?
13. Describe the significance of phytosomes in herbal medicine.
14. List three benefits of phytosomes over traditional herbal extracts.
15. What is the primary constituent of Ginkgo Biloba Tablets and its purpose?
16. Explain the role of phospholipids in phytosomes.
17. Describe the purpose of Milk Thistle Tablets.
18. What is the main component in Ashwagandha Tablets and its purpose?
19. How does the Green Tea Phytosome enhance antioxidant activity in the body?
20. Explain the benefit of silybin phytosome over conventional silymarin extracts.

Long Answer Type Questions (Subjective):

1. Describe the significance of herbal formulations in traditional systems of medicine. Highlight the various forms and their benefits.
2. Explain the steps involved in the basic method to prepare an herbal syrup. Highlight the significance of each step.
3. Discuss the importance of consulting a healthcare professional before starting any herbal remedies. Highlight potential risks and interactions.
4. Describe the concept and benefits of phytosomes in enhancing the bioavailability of herbal extracts.

5. Compare and contrast the benefits and uses of Triphala and Chyawanprash in Ayurveda.
6. Explain the roles of primary and secondary constituents in herbal formulations, using the Elderberry Syrup formulation as an example.
7. Describe the various conventional herbal mixtures mentioned and explain their purposes.
8. Discuss the significance of excipients in herbal tablets. Explain their role using the Ashwagandha Tablets as an example.
9. Elaborate on the benefits of phytosomes with specific examples like Curcumin Phytosome and Silybin Phytosome.
10. Discuss the various herbal formulations in Western Herbalism and their significance in treating various ailments.

Answer Key for MCQs:

1. (c) Neem
2. (a) Liu Wei Di Huang Wan
3. (c) Sedative and insomnia relief
4. (d) Injection
5. (d) Both a and b
6. (c) Thyme
7. (b) Vitamin C
8. (c) Withanolides
9. (c) Improved bioavailability
10. (b) Ginkgo Biloba Tablets
11. (b) Chyawanprash
12. (c) South Africa
13. (a) Immune-boosting

14.(b) Mild to moderate depression

15.(c) Phospholipids

16.(c) Curcumin

17.(d) Adrenal glands

18.(c) Elderberries

19.(c) Brandy or vodka

20.(b) Stimulate the immune system

CHAPTER - 9

EVALUATION OF DRUGS

Drug evaluation is defined as the determination of identity, purity and quality of a drug. Identity means the identification of the drugs, quality means the quantity of active constituents present and purity means the extent of foreign material present.

The evaluation of herbal drugs refers to the systematic assessment of herbal medicines to ensure their safety, efficacy, and quality. This process encompasses a range of activities, from the authentication of the source material (usually plant-based) to preclinical and, in some cases, clinical studies, followed by quality control and post-market surveillance. The objective is to ascertain that the herbal medicine is consistent in its composition and therapeutic effect, free from contaminants, and safe for consumption.

The evaluation of herbal drugs, also known as herbal medicines or phytomedicines, is slightly different from that of synthetic drugs due to their complex nature, multiple constituents, and traditional usage. However, like conventional drugs, the assessment of herbal drugs aims to ensure their safety, efficacy, and quality.

Here's a summarized process:

1. **Source Authentication:**
    a. The identification of the plant species is critical. It includes macroscopic and microscopic examination, and sometimes DNA barcoding, to confirm the authenticity of the plant species.
2. **Preclinical Studies:**
    a. **Phytochemical Analysis:** Determines the presence of major classes of compounds (e.g., alkaloids, flavonoids, tannins).

b. **Standardization:** This process ensures consistency in the preparation and production of herbal drugs. Methods like high-performance liquid chromatography (HPLC) or gas chromatography (GC) can be used to identify and quantify specific active compounds.
c. **Toxicological Studies:** These studies are conducted to determine the safety profile of the herbal drug. Both acute and chronic toxicity studies are performed, typically in animals, to understand any potential side effects or toxicities.

3. **Clinical Studies:**
   a. While many herbal drugs are used based on traditional knowledge without going through rigorous clinical trials, there is an increasing trend, especially in the Western world, to subject them to clinical evaluations similar to conventional drugs.
   b. The phases (I-IV) of clinical testing can be applied to herbal drugs as well. However, there might be more emphasis on Phase IV post-marketing surveillance due to the long-standing traditional use of many herbal medicines.

Clinical Phases:

Phase I: Initial testing in a small group of healthy volunteers to evaluate safety, dosage, and side effects.

Phase II: Testing in a larger group of patients to assess efficacy and further evaluate safety.

Phase III: Testing in an even larger group of patients to confirm effectiveness, monitor side effects, compare the drug to commonly used treatments, and gather information for safe use.

Phase IV: Post-marketing surveillance. After a drug has been approved and is on the market, this phase monitors its long-term effectiveness and ensures no unforeseen side effects appear in the broader population.

4. **Regulatory Review:**
   a. Regulatory standards for herbal drugs vary significantly from country to country. While some nations might accept traditional usage as evidence, others demand rigorous scientific data.
   b. In countries like the US, many herbal products are sold as dietary supplements, which have a different regulatory pathway than conventional drugs.
5. **Quality Control:**
   a. Given that herbs can be sourced from various regions and are subject to varying agricultural conditions, rigorous quality control is essential.
   b. This includes testing for contaminants such as heavy metals, pesticides, and microbial contamination.
6. **Post-marketing Surveillance:**
   a. Like synthetic drugs, herbal medicines are also monitored after they reach the market to ensure no unforeseen side effects appear in the broader population.
7. **Adverse Effects and Interactions:**
   a. It's a myth that all herbal drugs are safe because they are "natural". All medicines, including herbal ones, can have side effects. Furthermore, herbal drugs can interact with synthetic drugs or other herbs, potentially leading to increased or decreased drug effects or new side effects.
8. **Ethnopharmacological and Ethnobotanical Studies:**

a. These studies explore the traditional uses of plants by indigenous cultures. This knowledge can offer insights into potential therapeutic applications and safety considerations.

WHO GUIDELINES FOR THE ASSESSMENT OF HERBAL MEDICINES

The World Health Organization (WHO) provides a set of guidelines and recommendations to regulate and assess the quality, safety, and efficacy of herbal medicines. The general objectives are to ensure that herbal medicines are of good quality, safe, and effective and to assist and guide member states in developing their regulatory frameworks for herbal medicines. Here are the primary aspects of WHO's guidelines on herbal medicines:

1. **Quality Control:**
   a. WHO emphasizes the importance of meticulous quality control of herbal medicines, focusing on correct identification, purity, and content.
   b. It involves screening for contaminants, like heavy metals, pesticides, and microbiological contamination.
2. **Safety Assessment:**
   a. WHO recommends safety assessments, including thorough toxicity studies, to be conducted on herbal medicines to ascertain their safety.
   b. This involves documenting any adverse effects, interactions, contraindications, and precautions related to the use of the herbal medicine.
3. **Efficacy Assessment:**
   a. WHO advises on the evaluation of the efficacy of herbal medicines based on their traditional uses and, where available, on scientific research.
   b. Clinical trials, where feasible, should be conducted to validate the traditional use and to generate evidence on efficacy and dosing.

4. **Regulatory Framework:**
   a. WHO provides guidelines to assist member states in developing robust regulatory frameworks for the licensing, manufacturing, and distribution of herbal medicines.
   b. This includes regulations regarding labeling, advertising, and post-marketing surveillance of herbal medicines.
5. **Pharmacovigilance:**
   a. WHO emphasizes the importance of establishing systems for monitoring and reporting adverse drug reactions associated with herbal medicines.

International Council for Harmonisation

The International Council for Harmonisation of Technical Requirements for Pharmaceuticals for Human Use (ICH) primarily focuses on the harmonization of technical requirements for the registration of pharmaceutical products among its member regions (European Union, Japan, and the United States). Although the ICH's core guidelines target conventional pharmaceuticals, they have implications for herbal products, especially when herbal extracts or components are used as active pharmaceutical ingredients in conventional medicines.

As of my last update in January 2022, ICH has not released dedicated guidelines specifically for the assessment of herbal drugs, as the WHO has. However, herbal drugs integrated into pharmaceuticals can be assessed using the general ICH guidelines. Here's how some ICH guidelines may be applicable:

1. **Quality Guidelines:**
   a. **Q1 (Stability Testing):** Determines the shelf life and recommended storage conditions of the herbal drug.
   b. **Q2 (Validation of Analytical Procedures):** Helps ensure the methods used to analyze herbal drugs are validated and reliable.

c. **Q3 (Impurities):** Aims to regulate and limit impurities in the herbal drug, ensuring its purity and safety.

d. **Q5 (Quality of Biotechnological/Biological Products):** Might be applied in cases where the herbal product involves biotechnological processes.

2. **Safety Guidelines:**

   a. **S1 (Carcinogenicity Testing):** Ensures that the herbal drug doesn't promote cancer.

   b. **S2 (Genotoxicity Testing):** Assesses the potential for the herbal drug to damage genetic information within a cell.

   c. **S3 (Toxicokinetics and Pharmacokinetics):** Evaluates how the herbal drug behaves inside the body.

   d. **S4 (Toxicity Testing):** Provides general guidelines on the duration and conduct of chronic toxicity testing, which can apply to some herbal drugs.

3. **Efficacy Guidelines:**

   a. **E6 (Good Clinical Practice):** If clinical trials are conducted on an herbal drug, this guideline ensures ethical and quality standards.

   b. **E8 (General Considerations for Clinical Trials):** Offers guidance on designing, conducting, recording, and reporting clinical trials, which may include trials on herbal products.

While these guidelines can offer general directions for the evaluation of herbal drugs, there's a recognized need for specialized guidelines that consider the unique challenges and complexities associated with herbal products. However, manufacturers who wish to introduce herbal products as pharmaceuticals in ICH member regions often follow these guidelines to meet the rigorous safety, efficacy, and quality standards.

WHO GUIDELINES FOR STANDARDIZATION OF MEDICINAL PLANTS

1. **Botanical Evaluation:**
   a. **Sensory Evaluation:**
      i. Visual microscopy
      ii. Touch.
      iii. Odour.
      iv. Taste.
   b. **Foreign matter:**
      i. Foreign plants.
      ii. Foreign animals.
      iii. Foreign minerals, etc.
   c. **Microscopy:**
      i. Histological observation.
      ii. Histochemical detection
      iii. Measurements.
2. **Physiochemical evaluation:**
   a. Thin Layer Chromatography.
   b. Extractive matter
      i. Hot water soluble extractive value.
      ii. Cold water Extractive matter.
      iii. Ethanol extractive matter.
   c. Water content and volatile matter: LOD, Azeotropic.
   d. Volatile oils: By steam distillation.
3. **Pharmacological evaluation:**
   a. **Bitterness value:** Unit eq. to bitterness of standard solution of quinine hydrochloride.

b. **Haemolytic activity:** on Ox blood by comparison with standard reference saponin.
c. **Astringency:** Fraction (Tannins) that binds to standard hide powder.
d. **Swelling Index:** In Water.
e. **Foaming Index:** Foam height produced by 1 gm material under specified conditions.

4. **Toxicological evaluation:**
   a. **Pesticide residue:**
      i. Total organic chloride
      ii. Total organic phosphorous.
   b. **Arsenic:** Strain produced on $HgBr_2$ paper in comparison to standard stain.
   c. **Heavy metals:** Cadmium and lead.
5. **Microbiological Contamination:**
   a. Total viable aerobic count.
   b. **Pathogens:** Enterobacteriaceae, E. coli, Salmonella, P. aerogenosa and S. aureus.
   c. **Aflatoxins:** By TLC using standard Aflatoxins (B_1, B_2, G_1, G_2) mixture.
6. **Radioactive contamination.**

MACROSCOPICAL CHARACTERS

Macroscopic identity of medicinal plant materials is based on shape, size, colour, surface characteristics, texture, fracture characteristic and appearance of the cut surface.

6. **Size:** A graduated ruler in millimeters is adequate for the measurement of the length, width and thickness of crude materials. Small seeds and fruits may be

measured by aligning 10 of them on a sheet of calibrated paper, with 1 mm spacing between lines, and dividing the result by 10.

7. **Colour:** Examine the untreated sample under diffuse daylight may be used. The colour of the sample should be compared with that of a reference sample.
8. **Surface charactestics:** texture and fracture characteristics: Examine the untreated sample. If necessary, a magnifying lens may be used. Wetting with water or reagents, as required, may be necessary to observe the characteristics of a cut surface. Touch the material to determine if it is soft or hard; bend and rupture it to obtain information on brittleness and the appearance of the fracture plane- whether it is fibrous, smooth, rough and granular, etc.
9. **Odour:** If the material is expected to be innocuous, place a small portion of the sample in the palm of the hand or a beaker of suitable size, and slowly and repeatedly inhale the air over the material. If no distinct odour is perceptible, crush the sample between the thumb and index finger or between the palms of the hands using gentle pressure. If the material is known to be dangerous, crush by mechanical means and then pour a small quantity of boiling water onto the crushed sample in a beaker. First, determine the strength of the odour (none, weak, distinct, strong) and then the odour sensation (aromatic, fruity, musty, moldy, rancid, etc.). A direct comparison of the odour with a defined substance is advisable (e.g. peppermint should have an odour similar to menthol, clove a similar to eugenol).
10. **Taste:**

    Chirata: Bitter

    Glycyrrhiza: Sweet

    Lemon: Sour.

DETERMINATION OF SWELLING INDEX

Many plant materials are of specific therapeutic or pharmaceutical utility because of their swelling properties, especially gums and those containing an appreciable amount of mucilage, pectin or hemicelluloses.

Procedure: Weigh accurately 1 gm of plant material into a 25 ml glass stoppered measuring cylinder. The internal diameter of the cylinder should be about 16 mm, the length of the graduated portion about 125 mm, marked in 0.2 ml divisions from 0 to 25 ml in an upwards direction. Ad 25 ml of water and shake the mixture thoroughly every 10 minutes for 1 hr. allow to stand for 3 hrs at room temperature. Measure the volume in ml occupied by the plant material, including any sticky mucilage. Calculate the mean value of the individual determination.

DETERMINATION OF FOAMING INDEX

Plant materials contain saponins that can cause persistent foam, when an aqueous decoction is shaken.

Procedure: Weigh accurately 1 gm of coarse powder of plant material and transfer to a 500 ml conical flask containing 100 ml of boiling water. Maintain at moderate boiling for 30 minutes. Cool and filter into a 100 ml volumetric flask and add sufficient water through the filter to dilute to volume. Pour the decoction into 10 stoppered test tubes in successive portions 1ml, 2ml, 3ml, etc upto 10 ml, and adjust the volume of the liquid in each tube with water to 10 ml. stopper the tubes and shake them in a lengthwise motion for 15 seconds, two shakes per second. Allow to stand for 15 minutes and measure the height of the foam. If the height of the foam in every tube is less than 1 cm, the foaming index is less than 100. If a height of foam of 1 cm is measured in any tube, the volume of the plant material decoction in the tube (a) is used to determine the index. If this tube is the first or second tube in a series, prepare an intermediate dilution in a similar manner to obtain a more precise result. If the height of the foam is more than 1 cm in every tube, the foaming index is over 1000. in the case repeat the determination using a new series of dilutions of the decoction in order to obtain a result.

$$\text{Foaming Index} = \frac{1000}{a}$$

Where a = the volume in ml of the decoction used for preparing the dilution in the tube where foaming to a height of 1 cm is observed.

DETERMINATION OF MICROBIAL CONTAMINATIONS

1. **Test for Salmonella:**
    a. Take 10 gm of powdered material and make the volume up to 100 ml with lactose broth. The mixture is incubated at 35-37^{0}C for 4 hrs. A further 10 ml of this sample is taken. 100 ml of tetra methylene brilliant green bile broth is added to it and incubated at 37- 40^{0}C for 24 hrs. 1 ml sample is taken from it and planted on a xylose lysine deoxyxcholate agar media. Deoxyxcholate citrate agar or brilliant green agar can also be used. This is incubated at 35^{0}C for 50 hrs. Small transparent and colourless with an opaque, pink (Surrounded by a pink to red zone) zone indicates the presence of S. typhi.
    b. **Biochemical test:** The colonies obtained from the above culture are treated with polyvalent salmonella antisera. This is known as serotyping or slide agglutination test. Appearance of clumping of the cells confirms the presence of salmonella species.

2. **Test for E. coli:**

a. A drug is tested for the presence of E. coli by taking 10 gms of powdered material and making the volume up to 100 ml with lactose broth. This mixture should be incubated for 4 hrs at 35-37^{0}C. 1 ml sample from this is taken and serial dilutions are made with 9 ml of MacConkey broth of concentrations 100 mg/ml, 10 mg/ml, 0.1 mg/ml and 0.01 mg/ ml. theses samples are incubated at 37^{0}C for 18 hrs. a ml of each is incubated on MacConkey agar media, and further incubated for 24 hrs at 35-37^{0}C. Growth of red generally non-mucoid colonies of gram negative rods indicating the presence of E.coli.

3. **Test for Staphylococcus aureus:**
   a. Take 10 gm of powder material and make up the volume up to 100 ml with NA broth. This mixture is incubated at 35-37^{0}C for 4 hrs. One ml of this sample is plated on Baird- Parker agar media F, and incubated at 35-37^{0}C for 48 hrs. Black colonies of gram +ve cocci, surrounded by clear zones indicate the presence of Staphylococcus aureus.

DETERMINATION OF TANNINS

Tannins are substances capable of turning animal hides into leather by binding proteins to form water- insoluble substances that resistant to proteolytic enzymes. This process, when applied to living tissue, is known as an "astringent" action and is the reason for therapeutic application of tannins.

Method: Weigh accurately 10 gm of fine plant powder into a conical flask. Add 150 ml of water and heat over a boiling water- bath for 30 minutes. Cool, transfer the mixture to a 250 ml volumetric flask and dilute to volume with water. Allow the solid material to settle and filter the liquid through a filter- paper, diameter 12 cm, discarding the first 50 ml of the filtrate.

To determine the total amount of material that is extractable into water, evaporate 50 ml of the plant material extract to dryness, dry the residue in an oven at 105°C for 4 hrs and weigh (T_1).

To determine the amount of plant material not bound to hide powder and shake well for 60 minutes. Filter and evaporate 50 ml of the clear filtrate to dryness. Dry the residue in an oven at 105°C and weigh (T_2).

To determine the solubility of hide powder, take 6 gm of hide powder, add 80 ml of water and shake well for 60 minutes. Filter and evaporate 50 ml of the clear filtrate to dryness. Dry the residue in an oven at 105°C and weigh (T_0).

Calculate the quantity of tannins as percentage using the following formula:

$$\frac{[T_1 - (T_2 - T_0)] \times 500}{w}$$

Where w = the weight of the plant material in gms.

STABILITY TESTING OF HERBAL DRUGS

Stability testing of herbal drugs is crucial to ensure that the herbal product maintains its desired quality, safety, and efficacy throughout its shelf life. Given the complex nature of herbal drugs, which often contain multiple active constituents, stability testing can be more challenging compared to synthetic drugs.

Objectives of Stability Testing:

1. **Determine Shelf Life:** To define the period during which the herbal product meets all established specifications.
2. **Determine Storage Conditions:** To recommend optimal storage conditions to maintain the product's quality.

3. **Confirm Packaging Appropriateness:** To ensure the packaging provides adequate protection against identified external factors, such as moisture and light.

Factors Influencing Stability:

1. **Inherent Plant Factors:** Natural variance in plant materials due to genetics, growth conditions, harvesting time, etc.
2. **Processing Factors:** Techniques of extraction, purification, drying, and formulation can influence stability.
3. **External Factors:** Light, temperature, humidity, oxygen, and microbial contamination can affect stability.

Types of Stability Studies:

1. **Real-time Stability Studies:** The product is stored under recommended storage conditions, and the stability is tested at scheduled intervals.
2. **Accelerated Stability Studies:** The product is stored under conditions more strenuous than its recommended storage conditions (e.g., higher temperatures) to predict its stability in a shorter timeframe.
3. **Stress Testing:** The product is subjected to conditions beyond its tolerance to understand potential degradation pathways and to develop methods for stability studies.

Parameters Assessed in Stability Testing:

1. **Physical Stability:**
    a. Appearance, color, odor
    b. Particle size (for suspensions)
    c. Re-suspendability (for suspensions)
    d. Viscosity

e. pH

2. **Chemical Stability:**
   a. Concentration of main active compounds
   b. Presence of degradation products
   c. Any changes in the chemical profile using techniques like HPLC, GC, or TLC
3. **Microbiological Stability:**
   a. Total microbial count
   b. Absence/presence of specific pathogens
   c. Effectiveness of preservatives over time
4. **Therapeutic Stability:**
   a. Ensuring that the herbal drug maintains its therapeutic effect throughout its shelf life.
5. **Toxicological Stability:**
   a. Absence or presence of any new potentially harmful degradation products.

Challenges in Stability Testing of Herbal Drugs:

1. **Complexity of Herbal Preparations:** Due to multiple constituents, it can be challenging to monitor all potential changes.
2. **Lack of Marker Compounds:** Not all herbal medicines have identified active ingredients or marker compounds, making it challenging to standardize and monitor stability.
3. **Variability of Raw Materials:** Natural variance in plant materials can cause batch-to-batch variability.

Packaging and Storage:

The packaging plays a crucial role in the stability of herbal drugs. It protects the product from light, moisture, and microbial contamination. Proper labeling indicating storage conditions, expiration date, and other necessary details is crucial.

TYPES OF STABILITY STUDY:

Real-time stability studies

Real-time stability studies refer to the systematic evaluation of a pharmaceutical product's stability under the recommended storage conditions for the product's intended shelf life. These studies are conducted to determine how the quality of a drug varies over time under the influence of environmental factors like temperature, humidity, and light.

Objectives of Real-time Stability Studies:

1. **Determine Shelf Life:** Identify the expiration or use-by date for the product.
2. Validate Storage Conditions: Confirm the recommended storage conditions (e.g., "store below 25°C" or "refrigerate between 2°C to 8°C").
3. **Determine Packaging Adequacy:** Ensure the chosen packaging provides proper protection against potential external factors.
4. **Monitor Quality Over Time:** Assess any changes in the physical, chemical, and microbiological properties of the product.

Procedure for Real-time Stability Studies:

1. **Selection of Batches:** At least three batches of the product are typically selected, preferably of different scales or from different manufacturing sites.
2. **Storage Conditions:** The selected batches are stored under the recommended conditions specified for the product. This often includes the intended temperature and humidity settings.

3. **Sampling Frequency:** Samples are withdrawn at specified intervals over the study's duration, such as 0, 3, 6, 9, 12, 18, 24 months. The initial time point (0 month) provides a baseline.
4. **Testing Parameters:** At each time point, specific parameters are evaluated, which may include:
   a. **Physical parameters:** Appearance, odor, color, dissolution, and disintegration.
   b. **Chemical parameters:** Assay of the active ingredient, impurity levels, and pH.
   c. **Microbiological parameters:** Total microbial count and absence/presence of specific pathogens.
   d. **Other product-specific parameters:** Depending on the nature of the drug, additional tests like particle size distribution or viscosity might be included.
5. **Data Analysis:** The data collected over time is analyzed to identify trends or changes in the product's quality. Statistical tools can be employed to forecast the product's shelf life based on the observed changes.

Outcomes of Real-time Stability Studies:

1. **Expiration/Use-by Date Determination:** Based on the stability data, an expiration or use-by date is established.
2. **Post-approval Changes:** If there are any changes in the manufacturing process, formulation, or packaging, real-time stability studies can help determine the impact of these changes on the product's stability.
3. **Validation of Accelerated Stability Studies:** Data from real-time stability studies can validate predictions made using accelerated stability studies, which are conducted under more stressful conditions to estimate the product's stability in a shorter timeframe.

Challenges:

1. **Time-Consuming:** Since these studies span the product's intended shelf life, they can be lengthy.
2. **Storage Space:** Adequate facilities are required to store the samples under controlled conditions throughout the study.
3. **Changes in the Product Profile**: Unanticipated changes might occur, and their cause (e.g., formulation, process, packaging) must be identified and addressed.

Accelerated Stability Studies:

Accelerated stability studies involve assessing the stability of a product under conditions more severe than those of its intended storage environment. By exposing the product to elevated temperatures and often increased humidity levels, these studies aim to speed up any chemical, physical, or microbiological changes that might occur over time. The goal is to predict the product's long-term behavior in a shorter duration.

Objectives of Accelerated Stability Studies:

1. **Predict Shelf Life:** Estimate the expiration or use-by date for the product in a shorter time frame.
2. **Support Real-time Data:** Provide an early indication of long-term stability, especially useful for new products.
3. **Formulation Development:** Guide the development of new formulations by comparing the stability of different formulations under stressed conditions.
4. **Packaging Evaluation:** Assess the protective role of packaging under stressful conditions.

Procedure for Accelerated Stability Studies:

1. **Storage Conditions:** Products are stored at elevated temperatures, usually 10°C to 20°C higher than their intended storage temperatures. For instance, if a product is intended for storage at 25°C, it might be exposed to 40°C or even 50°C. Increased humidity levels (e.g., 75% RH) might also be applied, depending on the product and the study design.
2. **Sampling:** Similar to real-time stability studies, samples are withdrawn at specified intervals, but the duration is shorter. For example, samples might be tested at 0, 1, 2, 3, and 6 months.
3. **Testing Parameters:** At each sampling interval:
   a. **Physical parameters:** Appearance, color, odor, dissolution, and disintegration.
   b. **Chemical parameters:** Assay of the active ingredient, impurity levels, and pH.
   c. **Microbiological parameters:** Total microbial count and specific pathogens.
   d. **Other product-specific parameters:** Depending on the nature of the product, additional tests might be necessary.
4. **Data Analysis:** Any observed changes in the product are recorded. The rate of degradation can be determined, and using the Arrhenius equation or other relevant models, the product's shelf life under normal storage conditions can be extrapolated.

Limitations of Accelerated Stability Studies:

1. **Different Degradation Pathways:** The accelerated conditions might induce degradation pathways that wouldn't occur under normal storage conditions.

2. **Physical Changes**: Elevated temperatures might cause physical changes, like melting, that wouldn't be representative of the product's behavior at its intended storage temperature.
3. **Data Interpretation:** Extrapolating data to predict long-term stability has inherent uncertainties, and the predictions need to be validated by real-time stability studies.

Regulatory Perspective:

Many regulatory agencies, including the US FDA and the European Medicines Agency (EMA), rely on the International Council for Harmonisation (ICH) Q1A guidelines for stability testing. These guidelines provide specific conditions for conducting accelerated stability studies for various types of products and regions, considering factors like temperature, humidity, and light.

STRESS TESTING

Stress testing, in the context of stability studies, is designed to evaluate the inherent stability of a molecule or product by exposing it to conditions that are more extreme than those used in accelerated stability testing. The primary goal is to understand the degradation pathways and to identify potential degradation products of the drug substance or drug product.

Objectives of Stress Testing:

1. **Determine Inherent Stability:** Understand the chemical, physical, and microbiological stability of the molecule.
2. **Identify Degradation Pathways:** Determine how the drug might degrade under various conditions, providing insight into potential vulnerabilities.

3. **Identify Degradation Products:** Characterize any breakdown products formed during degradation. This is essential for safety since degradation products can have different toxicological profiles.
4. **Validate Analytical Methods:** Ensure that the analytical methods used in stability testing can detect and differentiate between the drug and its degradation products.

Conditions Used in Stress Testing:

1. **Thermal Degradation:** Expose the drug to temperatures much higher than those used in accelerated studies. This can identify vulnerabilities to heat.
2. **Photolytic Degradation:** Expose the drug to direct sunlight or specific light wavelengths to understand its photosensitivity.
3. **Hydrolytic Degradation:** Expose the drug to varying pH levels to simulate conditions of extreme acidity or alkalinity.
4. **Oxidative Degradation:** Expose the drug to oxidizing agents to understand its stability in the presence of oxygen or other oxidative conditions.
5. **Mechanical Stress:** For certain dosage forms, like emulsions or suspensions, mechanical stresses such as shaking or stirring might be applied.

Procedure for Stress Testing:

1. **Sample Preparation:** Samples of the drug substance or product are prepared for exposure.
2. **Condition Exposure**: Samples are subjected to the stress conditions, often in a stepwise increasing manner to identify thresholds of degradation.
3. **Analysis:** At specified intervals, samples are removed and analyzed to detect any changes in the drug and identify degradation products. Techniques like HPLC, GC, MS, and NMR can be used.

4. **Evaluation:** The results are evaluated to determine the degradation pathways, identify degradation products, and understand the inherent stability of the molecule.

Implications and Considerations:

1. **Formulation Development:** Insights from stress testing can guide formulation strategies to enhance the stability of the drug product.
2. **Packaging Decisions:** If the drug is photosensitive, for instance, opaque or amber-colored packaging may be necessary.
3. **Storage Recommendations:** The findings can influence storage conditions and precautions mentioned on the product label.
4. **Safety and Toxicology:** Degradation products identified during stress testing might need to be evaluated for safety.

Regulatory Perspective:

Regulatory guidelines, such as those provided by the International Council for Harmonisation (ICH) in its Q1A(R2) document, provide guidance on the conduct and objectives of stress testing. The results of stress testing are a vital component of regulatory submissions, as they provide evidence of understanding the stability aspects of the drug substance and product.

Multiple Choice Questions (MCQs):

1. Drug evaluation primarily involves the determination of:
   a) Identity, purity, and quantity
   b) Identity, purity, and quality
   c) Quality, quantity, and source
   d) Source, identity, and quantity

2. Herbal drug evaluation is essential to ensure:
   a) Taste, flavor, and aroma
   b) Source, preparation, and usage
   c) Safety, efficacy, and quality
   d) Tradition, history, and popularity
3. What is the primary aim of source authentication in herbal drug evaluation?
   a) Understand the traditional uses of the plant
   b) Identify the specific region where the plant was grown
   c) Confirm the authenticity of the plant species
   d) Understand the chemical composition of the plant
4. In the preclinical studies of herbal drugs, which method is NOT used for standardization?
   a) DNA barcoding
   b) Gas chromatography (GC)
   c) High-performance liquid chromatography (HPLC)
   d) Phytochemical analysis
5. Which phase of clinical testing focuses on post-marketing surveillance?
   a) Phase I
   b) Phase II
   c) Phase III
   d) Phase IV
6. According to WHO guidelines, which of the following is NOT an aspect of herbal medicines assessment?
   a) Quality control
   b) Price control
   c) Safety assessment
   d) Efficacy assessment

7. Which organization primarily focuses on the harmonization of technical requirements for pharmaceutical products among its member regions?
   a) WHO
   b) ICH
   c) UNICEF
   d) FDA
8. In the WHO guidelines for standardization of medicinal plants, the method to measure bitterness value involves comparing with:
   a) Standard solution of glucose
   b) Standard solution of menthol
   c) Standard solution of quinine hydrochloride
   d) Standard solution of sodium chloride
9. In the macroscopical characters of medicinal plant materials, what provides a baseline for comparisons?
   a) Size and weight
   b) Sensory evaluation
   c) Chemical composition
   d) Therapeutic properties
10. Real-time stability studies aim to:
   a) Predict the product's long-term behavior in a shorter duration
   b) Understand the degradation pathways and potential degradation products
   c) Evaluate a product's stability under recommended storage conditions
   d) Assess the stability of a molecule under extreme conditions
11. Which of the following is NOT an outcome of real-time stability studies?
   a) Expiration date determination
   b) Determination of mechanical strength of the product
   c) Post-approval changes

d) Validation of accelerated stability studies

12. Accelerated stability studies are conducted to:

a) Validate real-time stability study predictions

b) Predict the shelf life of the product in a shorter time frame

c) Determine the drug's inherent stability

d) Identify the drug's reaction to mechanical stress

13. In stress testing, exposing a drug to direct sunlight or specific light wavelengths helps understand its:

a) Thermosensitivity

b) Photosensitivity

c) Oxidative resistance

d) Hydrolytic stability

14. Stress testing results can influence all of the following EXCEPT:

a) Formulation strategies

b) Packaging decisions

c) Storage recommendations

d) Drug pricing decisions

15. The primary purpose of stress testing is to:

a) Test the drug's performance under normal conditions

b) Evaluate the drug's resistance to mechanical stress

c) Understand the inherent stability of a molecule or product

d) Determine the drug's market value

16. In the context of drug evaluation, what does "identity" refer to?

a) Quantity of active constituents

b) Therapeutic effect of the drug

c) Identification of the drugs

d) Extent of foreign material present

17. Which phase of clinical testing primarily tests in a small group of healthy volunteers to evaluate safety, dosage, and side effects?

a) Phase I

b) Phase II

c) Phase III

d) Phase IV

18. ICH guidelines that might apply to the assessment of herbal drugs when used as active pharmaceutical ingredients in conventional medicines focus primarily on:

a) Herbal traditions

b) Technical requirements for registration

c) Ethnopharmacological studies

d) Traditional usage as evidence

19. Which test is used to determine the presence of Salmonella in a drug?

a) Test for E. coli

b) Test for Staphylococcus aureus

c) Test for Salmonella

d) Determination of tannins

20. In the determination of foaming index, a foaming index less than 100 is indicated when:

a) The height of the foam in every tube is more than 1 cm

b) The height of the foam in every tube is less than 1 cm

c) Only one tube has foam of less than 1 cm

d) Only one tube has foam of more than 1 cm

Short Answer Type Questions (Subjective)

1. Define drug evaluation in the context of herbal medicines.
2. Describe the process of source authentication in herbal drug evaluation.

3. What are the primary objectives of the WHO guidelines for the assessment of herbal medicines?
4. Why is the evaluation of herbal drugs different from that of synthetic drugs?
5. Explain the significance of preclinical studies in the evaluation of herbal drugs.
6. Why is post-marketing surveillance important for herbal medicines?
7. Describe the role of ethnopharmacological and ethnobotanical studies in the evaluation of herbal drugs.
8. What is the significance of the International Council for Harmonisation in the context of herbal drugs?
9. Describe the importance of macroscopical characters in the evaluation of medicinal plants.
10. What is the significance of the determination of foaming index in plant materials?
11. Explain the procedure for the determination of microbial contaminations in herbal drugs.
12. Why is stability testing crucial for herbal drugs?
13. Describe the objectives of accelerated stability studies.
14. What are the implications of stress testing in the stability studies of herbal drugs?
15. How do processing factors influence the stability of herbal drugs?
16. Why is the packaging critical in the stability of herbal drugs?
17. Explain the significance of the swelling index in the evaluation of plant materials.
18. Describe the impact of external factors on the stability of herbal drugs.
19. Why is the determination of tannins important in herbal drugs?
20. Explain the role of the International Council for Harmonisation in the evaluation of herbal drugs.

Long Answer Type Questions (Subjective)

1. Discuss in detail the process of the evaluation of herbal drugs, highlighting the importance of each step.
2. Describe the challenges faced in the evaluation of herbal drugs in comparison to synthetic drugs.
3. Elaborate on the role of WHO guidelines in ensuring the safety, efficacy, and quality of herbal medicines.
4. Discuss the significance of stability studies in the evaluation of herbal drugs, including the various types of stability studies.
5. Describe the importance of source authentication in the evaluation of herbal drugs and its impact on the final product.
6. Discuss the factors influencing the stability of herbal drugs, and explain the measures taken to ensure their stability.
7. Elaborate on the significance of the International Council for Harmonisation in regulating herbal medicines on a global scale.
8. Describe the process of phytochemical analysis in the evaluation of herbal drugs and its importance.
9. Discuss the relevance of macroscopic and microscopic evaluation in the assessment of medicinal plants.
10. Explain the role of preclinical and clinical studies in the evaluation of herbal drugs, highlighting their significance.

Answer Key:

1. b) Identity, purity, and quality
2. c) Safety, efficacy, and quality
3. c) Confirm the authenticity of the plant species
4. a) DNA barcoding
5. d) Phase IV

6. b) Price control
7. b) ICH
8. c) Standard solution of quinine hydrochloride
9. b) Sensory evaluation
10. c) Evaluate a product's stability under recommended storage conditions
11. b) Determination of mechanical strength of the product
12. b) Predict the shelf life of the product in a shorter time frame
13. b) Photosensitivity
14. d) Drug pricing decisions
15. c) Understand the inherent stability of a molecule or product
16. c) Identification of the drugs
17. a) Phase I
18. b) Technical requirements for registration
19. c) Test for Salmonella
20. b) The height of the foam in every tube is less than 1 cm

CHAPTER - 10

PATENTING OF NATURAL PRODUCTS

Patenting refers to the process by which individuals or entities obtain exclusive rights to an invention or innovation. For natural products:

1. **Novelty:** The substance or its use must be previously undisclosed and not part of the public domain.
2. **Non-obviousness/Inventive Step:** The natural product or its application should represent an innovation not evident to experts in the field.
3. **Utility:** The natural product must have a credible and specific use.
4. **Enablement:** The patent application should provide enough details for an expert in the field to reproduce the invention.
5. **Nature-derived vs. Naturally Occurring:** Merely isolating a substance from nature doesn't make it patentable. However, modifications or specific applications of naturally occurring substances might be patentable.

Regulatory requirements for natural products

Regulatory requirements pertain to the rules and guidelines set by governmental agencies that oversee the safety, efficacy, and marketing of drugs, supplements, and other health-related products. For natural products:

1. **Identity and Quality:** Regulatory bodies require proof of consistent quality and identity, often through chemical profiling and specification of marker compounds.
2. **Safety:** The safety profile of the product needs to be established, potentially through toxicological studies and human trials.
3. Efficacy: If marketed as a drug, clinical trials demonstrating the product's efficacy for a particular condition or disease are essential.

4. Drug vs. Supplement Distinction: Some jurisdictions allow marketing of natural products as dietary supplements without clinical trials, but disease-related claims cannot be made.
5. Traditional Use: Some regions have provisions for products with long-established traditional use, requiring lesser clinical data but still demanding safety and quality evidence.
6. Manufacturing Standards: Compliance with Good Manufacturing Practices (GMP) is mandatory to ensure consistent production and quality.
7. Labeling and Marketing: Product claims must be accurate and evidence-based, with clear indications, uses, and potential side effects.

Natural products, which include plant extracts, marine organisms, microorganisms, and other naturally derived substances, have long been a source of therapeutic agents and pharmaceuticals. When it comes to patenting and regulatory requirements, natural products occupy a unique space. Here's an overview:

Patenting requirements for natural products

1. **Novelty:** The natural product or its use must be new. If the substance has been previously described or used in the public domain, it cannot be patented.
2. Non-obviousness/Inventive Step: The natural product or its application should not be obvious to a person skilled in the art based on existing knowledge.
3. Utility: The natural product must have a specific and credible utility. Merely isolating a compound from nature is not sufficient; the compound's functional application or therapeutic use needs to be demonstrated.
4. Enablement: The patent application should provide sufficient details so that a person skilled in the field can reproduce the invention without undue experimentation.

5. Nature-derived vs. Naturally Occurring: Post the U.S. Supreme Court decision in the "Myriad Genetics" case, naturally occurring DNA sequences, as they exist in nature, are not patentable. However, modifications of these sequences or methods of using them can be. Similar principles apply to other naturally occurring substances; merely isolating them is not sufficient for patent protection, but modifications or specific applications might be.

DEFINITIONS FOR THE SPECIFIED TERMS:

Patent:

Definition: A patent is a form of intellectual property that grants the patent holder exclusive rights to an invention for a limited period, typically 20 years from the filing date. In exchange, the inventor provides a detailed public disclosure of the invention. This right prevents others from making, using, selling, and distributing the patented innovation without the patent holder's consent.

IPR (Intellectual Property Rights):

Definition: Intellectual Property Rights (IPR) refer to the legal rights granted to innovators, creators, and inventors over their creations or inventions. These rights can include patents, copyrights, trademarks, trade secrets, and more. IPR provides protection, allowing the holder to control the use of the intellectual property and potentially benefit financially from it.

Farmer's Right:

Definition: Farmers' rights recognize the contributions of farmers in conserving, improving, and making available plant genetic resources. These rights empower farmers to save, use, exchange, and sell farm-saved seeds and propagating material. The exact provisions and extent of farmers' rights may vary by country and the specific treaties they've ratified.

Breeder's Right (Plant Breeder's Right):

Definition: Plant breeder's rights, also known as plant variety rights, are a form of intellectual property rights that grant plant breeders protection for their new plant varieties. With this protection, breeders can prevent others from selling, producing, or reproducing their variety without their consent for a set number of years.

Bioprospecting:

Definition: Bioprospecting is the exploration of natural sources for small molecules, genes, or other valuable resources with potential commercial applications, especially in pharmaceuticals or agriculture. It often involves studying indigenous knowledge about the use of plants, animals, and microorganisms.

Biopiracy:

Definition: Biopiracy refers to the unauthorized and uncompensated extraction and commercialization of biological resources or related traditional knowledge from indigenous communities or nations. Biopiracy often occurs when external entities exploit natural resources or traditional knowledge without proper permission, sharing of benefits, or acknowledgment of the source community or nation.

Patent:

A patent is a legal right granted by a government to an inventor or their assignee, giving them the exclusive right to make, use, sell, and distribute an invention for a certain period of time. Patents are a crucial component of intellectual property law and are intended to encourage innovation by providing inventors with protection for their new inventions.

Types of Patents

1. Utility Patents:
    - Purpose: Protect new and useful processes, machines, manufactures, or compositions of matter.

- Duration: Typically 20 years from the filing date.

2. Design Patents:
   - Purpose: Protect new, original, and ornamental designs for an article of manufacture.
   - Duration: Typically 15 years from the date of grant.
3. Plant Patents:
   - Purpose: Protect new and distinct, invented, or discovered asexually reproduced plant varieties.
   - Duration: Typically 20 years from the filing date.

Advantages of Patents

1) Exclusive Rights:
   a) Market Control: Patents give inventors exclusive rights to their invention, allowing them to control its use and distribution.
   b) Competitive Advantage: This exclusivity can provide a significant competitive edge in the market.
2) Return on Investment:
   a) Monetization: Inventors can monetize their patents through licensing, selling, or commercializing the patented technology, potentially generating significant revenue.
3) Encouragement of Innovation:
   a) Incentive to Innovate: Patents encourage inventors to invest time and resources into developing new technologies by providing a period of exclusivity to recoup their investment.
4) Legal Protection:

a) Infringement Safeguard: Patents provide legal protection against unauthorized use, copying, or sale of the patented invention, enabling inventors to enforce their rights.

5) Market Position:

a) Brand Reputation: Holding patents can enhance a company's reputation as an innovator and leader in its field, potentially attracting investors and customers.

Disadvantages of Patents

1. Cost:
   a. Expense: Obtaining a patent can be costly, involving fees for filing, prosecution, and maintenance, as well as legal costs for preparing and defending the patent.
   b. Ongoing Costs: There are also maintenance fees to keep the patent in force.
2. Disclosure:
   a. Public Disclosure: Patent applications require full disclosure of the invention, which becomes publicly accessible. Competitors can access this information and potentially design around the patent.
3. Limited Duration:
   a. Time Limitation: Patents provide protection for a limited time (usually 20 years), after which the invention enters the public domain.
4. Complex Process:
   a. Time-Consuming: The patent application process can be lengthy and complex, often taking several years to obtain approval.
   b. Uncertainty: There is no guarantee that a patent will be granted, even after substantial investment in the application process.

5. Enforcement Challenges:
    a. Litigation: Enforcing patent rights can involve costly and time-consuming legal battles if infringement occurs.
    b. Global Differences: Patent laws vary by country, and securing patent protection internationally requires navigating multiple legal systems and incurring additional costs.

Intellectual Property Rights (IPR)

Intellectual Property Rights (IPR) refer to the legal protections granted to the creators of intellectual property (IP), which includes inventions, literary and artistic works, designs, symbols, names, and images used in commerce. These rights are intended to encourage creativity and innovation by ensuring that creators can reap the benefits of their creations.

Types of Intellectual Property Rights

1) Patents:
    a) Protects: Inventions and discoveries.
    b) Duration: Generally 20 years from the filing date for utility patents; 15 years from the grant date for design patents.
    c) Example: A new pharmaceutical drug.
2) Trademarks:
    a) Protects: Symbols, names, and slogans used to identify goods and services.
    b) Duration: Indefinitely, as long as the trademark is in use and properly maintained.
    c) Example: The Nike swoosh logo.
3) Copyrights:
    a) Protects: Literary and artistic works such as books, music, films, and software.

b) Duration: Typically the life of the author plus 70 years (varies by jurisdiction).

c) Example: A novel or a song.

4) Trade Secrets:

a) Protects: Confidential business information that provides a competitive edge.

b) Duration: Indefinite, as long as the information remains confidential.

c) Example: The formula for Coca-Cola.

5) Industrial Designs:

a) Protects: The aesthetic aspect of objects, such as the design of a chair or a car.

b) Duration: Varies by country, typically around 10-25 years.

c) Example: The unique design of a smartphone.

6) Geographical Indications (GIs):

a) Protects: Names or signs used on products with a specific geographical origin and qualities or reputation.

b) Duration: Indefinite, as long as the product maintains its unique characteristics.

c) Example: Champagne from the Champagne region in France.

Advantages of Intellectual Property Rights

1) Encouragement of Innovation and Creativity:

a) Incentives: By providing exclusive rights, IPRs encourage individuals and companies to invest time and resources in creating new products and ideas.

2) Economic Benefits:

a) Monetization: Creators can monetize their IP through licensing, sales, or commercialization, generating revenue and economic growth.

3) Market Differentiation:
   a) Brand Protection: Trademarks and design rights help businesses differentiate their products from competitors, building brand identity and loyalty.
4) Legal Protection:
   a) Enforcement: IPRs provide legal means to prevent unauthorized use, copying, or distribution of IP, protecting the creator's investment.
5) Encouragement of Investment:
   a) Attracts Investment: Strong IP protection can attract investors and partners, as it demonstrates the value and uniqueness of the IP.

Disadvantages of Intellectual Property Rights

1) High Costs:
   a) Expense: Securing and maintaining IPRs can be costly, involving application fees, legal fees, and enforcement costs.
   b) Ongoing Costs: Maintenance fees and potential litigation expenses add to the financial burden.
2) Limited Duration:
   a) Expiration: IPRs are not permanent and eventually expire, after which the protected work or invention enters the public domain.
3) Complexity:
   a) Legal Complexity: Navigating the IPR system can be complex and time-consuming, requiring specialized legal expertise.
   b) International Variations: Different countries have different IP laws, making international protection challenging and expensive.
4) Potential for Abuse:
   a) Monopolistic Practices: IPRs can be used to create monopolies, potentially stifling competition and innovation.

b) Patent Trolls: Entities that acquire patents solely to sue others for infringement without intending to develop the patented technology.

5) Barriers to Access:

a) Access Issues: Strong IPRs can limit access to important technologies, medicines, and information, particularly in developing countries.

Breeder's Right (Plant Breeder's Right)

Plant Breeder's Rights (PBR), also known as Plant Variety Protection (PVP), are a form of intellectual property rights specifically granted to the breeders of new plant varieties. These rights are intended to encourage the development of new plant varieties by providing breeders with exclusive control over the propagation material (seeds, cuttings, divisions, tissue culture) of their new plant variety for a certain period.

Key Features of Breeder's Rights

1) Eligibility:

a) Novelty: The plant variety must be new, meaning it has not been commercially exploited for more than one year in the country of application.

b) Distinctness: The variety must be clearly distinguishable from any other known variety.

c) Uniformity: The variety must be sufficiently uniform in its relevant characteristics.

d) Stability: The variety must remain consistent in its essential characteristics through successive generations.

2) Scope of Protection:

a) Exclusive Rights: The breeder has exclusive rights to produce, reproduce, sell, import, and export the protected variety.

b) Duration: Typically, 20 to 25 years for most crops, and up to 30 years for trees and vines, depending on the country and specific regulations.

3) Farmers' Privilege:

a) Exemptions: In many jurisdictions, farmers are allowed to save and replant seeds from protected varieties on their own holdings, although they may not sell the seeds without the breeder's permission.

4) Breeder's Exemption:

a) Use in Breeding: Other breeders can use protected varieties for further breeding and research without the consent of the original breeder, ensuring ongoing innovation.

Advantages of Breeder's Rights

1) Encouragement of Innovation:

a) Incentive to Develop New Varieties: By providing exclusive rights, PBR incentivizes breeders to invest in the development of new, improved plant varieties.

2) Economic Benefits:

a) Revenue Generation: Breeders can generate income through the sale of seeds and propagation material, as well as through licensing agreements.

b) Market Expansion: Protection can facilitate access to international markets, providing opportunities for broader commercial exploitation.

3) Agricultural Advancement:

a) Improved Varieties: PBR encourages the development of varieties with better yield, disease resistance, climate resilience, and other desirable traits, contributing to agricultural productivity and sustainability.

4) Legal Protection:

a) Enforcement: PBR provides legal means to prevent unauthorized reproduction and sale of protected varieties, safeguarding breeders' investments.

Disadvantages of Breeder's Rights

1) High Costs:
   a) Application and Maintenance: The process of applying for and maintaining PBR can be expensive, potentially limiting access for small breeders.
   b) Enforcement Costs: Legal action to enforce rights can be costly and time-consuming.
2) Limited Duration:
   a) Expiration: PBR is granted for a limited period, after which the variety enters the public domain and can be freely used by others.
3) Complexity:
   a) Regulatory Burden: The application process can be complex, requiring substantial documentation and compliance with specific criteria.
   b) Variability Across Jurisdictions: Different countries have different PBR laws and regulations, complicating international protection.
4) Access Issues:
   a) Farmer Impact: In some regions, the enforcement of PBR can restrict farmers' traditional practices of saving and replanting seeds, potentially increasing their dependence on commercial seed suppliers.
5) Potential for Abuse:
   a) Biopiracy: There are concerns about biopiracy, where breeders might obtain PBR for plant varieties derived from traditional knowledge or genetic resources without fair compensation to the communities that developed them.

Bioprospecting

Bioprospecting is the process of searching for, collecting, and utilizing biological materials from nature, such as plants, animals, and microorganisms, for commercially valuable genetic and biochemical properties. These materials can be used in a wide range of industries, including pharmaceuticals, agriculture, cosmetics, and biotechnology.

Key Aspects of Bioprospecting

1) Identification and Collection:
   a) Source of Biological Materials: Researchers identify and collect specimens from various ecosystems, including forests, oceans, and deserts.
   b) Targeted Species: The focus is often on species known or suspected to have valuable medicinal, agricultural, or industrial properties.
2) Screening and Research:
   a) Laboratory Analysis: Collected samples are analyzed to identify useful genetic or biochemical compounds.
   b) Development: Promising compounds are further researched and developed into products such as drugs, agricultural chemicals, or biotechnological tools.
3) Commercialization:
   a) Product Development: Successful bioprospecting leads to the development and commercialization of new products.
   b) Intellectual Property: Patents and other forms of IP protection are often sought to secure exclusive rights to the discoveries.

Advantages of Bioprospecting

1) Medical and Pharmaceutical Advances:

a) New Drugs: Many important drugs, such as antibiotics and anticancer agents, have been discovered through bioprospecting.
b) Treatment of Diseases: It can lead to new treatments for a wide range of diseases and health conditions.

2) Economic Benefits:
a) Revenue Generation: Commercial products developed through bioprospecting can generate significant revenue.
b) Local Economies: Bioprospecting projects can benefit local economies through job creation and infrastructure development.

3) Conservation Incentives:
a) Biodiversity Protection: The potential economic value of biodiversity can provide incentives for conservation and sustainable use of natural resources.

4) Scientific Knowledge:
a) Increased Understanding: Bioprospecting contributes to scientific knowledge about ecosystems, species, and their potential uses.

Disadvantages of Bioprospecting

1) Ethical and Legal Issues:
a) Biopiracy: There are concerns about biopiracy, where biological resources are exploited without proper authorization or compensation to the indigenous communities who have traditionally used these resources.
b) Access and Benefit Sharing: Ensuring fair and equitable sharing of benefits arising from the use of genetic resources is a major challenge.

2) Environmental Impact:
a) Resource Exploitation: Unsustainable bioprospecting practices can lead to overharvesting and depletion of natural resources.

b) Habitat Disruption: Collecting specimens can disrupt local ecosystems and wildlife habitats.

3) Regulatory Hurdles:

a) Complex Regulations: Navigating the legal frameworks governing bioprospecting, which can vary significantly between countries, is complex and time-consuming.

b) Compliance Costs: The cost of ensuring compliance with environmental and access regulations can be high.

4) Cultural Sensitivity:

a) Indigenous Knowledge: Misappropriation of traditional knowledge without consent or proper acknowledgment can lead to cultural insensitivity and exploitation.

PATENTING ASPECTS OF TRADITIONAL KNOWLEDGE AND NATURAL PRODUCTS

Patenting aspects of Traditional Knowledge (TK) and Natural Products (NPs) is a complex and sensitive area that intersects the realms of intellectual property, indigenous rights, commerce, and bioprospecting. The key issues and considerations include:

1. Traditional Knowledge:

a. **Definition:** TK refers to the collective wisdom, knowledge, and practices of indigenous communities accumulated over generations and intertwined with their cultural identity.

b. Patenting Issues:

i. **Novelty and Prior Art:** In many intellectual property systems, for something to be patented, it must be novel. Since TK is often passed down through generations and is orally transmitted, proving its prior existence can be challenging.

ii. **Documentation:** Some countries have developed Traditional Knowledge Digital Libraries (TKDL) to document TK and prevent its wrongful patenting by external entities.

iii. **Benefit Sharing:** If TK leads to commercial benefits, there's an ethical and sometimes legal imperative to share these benefits with the source community.

2. **Natural Products:**
   a. **Definition:** NPs are chemical compounds or substances produced by living organisms, often having potential therapeutic properties.
   b. **Patenting Issues:**
      i. **Nature-derived vs. Naturally Occurring:** After key legal decisions, like the "Myriad Genetics" case in the U.S., naturally occurring substances can't be patented. However, if a natural product is modified to yield a novel compound, or if a novel use is found, it may be patentable.
      ii. **Bioprospecting:** When entities search for NPs with commercial potential, it's crucial they obtain prior informed consent from local communities or nations and ensure fair benefit-sharing arrangements.
      iii. **Isolation and Purification:** Historically, isolated or purified forms of natural products were patentable in many jurisdictions. However, the acceptability of these patents varies and is evolving.

General Considerations:

1. **Access and Benefit Sharing (ABS):** The Nagoya Protocol, an international agreement, provides a framework for the fair and equitable sharing of benefits

arising from the utilization of genetic resources, which includes NPs derived from them.

2. **Disclosure of Source:** Some jurisdictions require patent applicants to disclose the source of genetic resources and TK used in their invention, ensuring transparency and adherence to ABS agreements.
3. **Opposition to Wrongful Patents:** With the documentation of TK, nations or indigenous communities can oppose or revoke patents that wrongfully capitalize on their TK without permission or benefit sharing.
4. **Cultural Sensitivity:** Beyond legal considerations, respecting the cultural significance of TK and associated natural resources is crucial. Commercial exploitation might sometimes be seen as disrespectful or a form of cultural appropriation.

CURCUMA (TURMERIC) CASE STUDY:

Background:

Turmeric, derived from the rhizome of the plant *Curcuma longa*, has been traditionally used in India for thousands of years, both as a culinary spice and for its medicinal properties. It's extensively documented in ancient Ayurvedic texts for its healing properties, particularly its ability to heal wounds and rashes.

The Controversial Patent:

1. In 1995, the U.S. Patent and Trademark Office (USPTO) granted a patent (Patent No. 5,401,504) to the University of Mississippi Medical Center. The patent was for a method to heal wounds using a composition that had turmeric (curcumin) as a key ingredient.
2. The stated innovation was the "use of turmeric in wound healing." Given the longstanding traditional use of turmeric in India for this exact purpose, many viewed this as a patent on a well-known traditional practice.

The Opposition:

1. The Indian Council of Scientific and Industrial Research (CSIR) challenged the patent. CSIR argued that there was no novelty in the "invention" since turmeric's wound-healing properties were well known and documented in traditional Indian medicinal systems.
2. To make its case, CSIR provided evidence from ancient Ayurvedic texts and other literature proving the prior use of turmeric for wound healing in India.

The Outcome:

In 1997, the USPTO agreed with the arguments presented by CSIR and revoked the patent, accepting that turmeric's therapeutic properties were indeed a part of the prior art, making the patent claim non-novel and hence non-patentable.

Significance & Implications:

1. The turmeric patent case became a landmark event in the discourse on traditional knowledge and intellectual property rights.
2. It highlighted the potential vulnerabilities of traditional knowledge to biopiracy and underscored the need to document and protect such knowledge. This case was instrumental in the development of the Traditional Knowledge Digital Library (TKDL) by India, which aimed to document traditional medicinal knowledge and prevent undue patent claims.
3. The case also emphasized the importance of vigilance by nations to protect their traditional knowledge from wrongful exploitation and the need for an international framework to guide the use of traditional knowledge and ensure fair benefit-sharing.

NEEM (*AZADIRACHTA INDICA*) CASE STUDY

Background:

The neem tree, scientifically known as *Azadirachta indica*, is indigenous to the Indian subcontinent. For thousands of years, various parts of the neem tree have been used in traditional Indian medicine for their therapeutic properties. It's often referred to as the "village pharmacy" in India because of its wide array of medicinal uses. Moreover, neem extracts have been traditionally used as biopesticides for their ability to deter pests.

The Controversial Patents:

1. Over the years, numerous patents were granted internationally on various uses and formulations of neem, especially in the US and Europe.
2. One of the most controversial patents was granted by the European Patent Office (EPO) in 1995 to the United States Department of Agriculture and the company W.R. Grace. The patent (EP 0436257 B1) was for a method to control fungi on plants using a hydrophobic extracted neem oil.

The Opposition:

1. The patent was challenged by a coalition that included the Indian environmental activist Vandana Shiva, the International Federation of Organic Agriculture Movements (IFOAM), and the European Green Party.
2. The main argument against the patent was that the fungicidal properties of neem were well-known in Indian traditional knowledge, and thus the patent lacked novelty.

The Outcome:

After a legal battle, in 2000, the EPO revoked the patent, ruling that the process for which the patent had been granted had already been in use in India, thus making the invention not novel.

Significance & Implications:

1. The neem case, similar to the turmeric case, became a symbol of the struggle against biopiracy and the unfair appropriation of traditional knowledge without due compensation.
2. It highlighted the need for clearer guidelines on patenting natural products and processes related to traditional knowledge.
3. The case also accentuated the importance of documentation of traditional knowledge, leading to initiatives like the Traditional Knowledge Digital Library (TKDL) in India, which documents traditional medicinal knowledge to prevent undue patent claims.
4. The revocation of the neem patent renewed discussions on access and benefit-sharing, leading to international frameworks such as the Nagoya Protocol.

MCQs (Objective)

1. What does a patent grant its holder?
   a) Temporary rights to an invention.
   b) Exclusive rights to an invention for a specific period.
   c) The right to use someone else's invention.
   d) Indefinite rights to an invention.
2. Which one of the following is NOT a patenting requirement for natural products?
   a) Novelty
   b) Non-obviousness/Inventive Step
   c) Utility
   d) Affordability
3. Which of the following is true about naturally occurring substances in the context of patenting?
   a) They are always patentable.

b) They are never patentable.

c) Isolating them makes them patentable.

d) Modifications or specific applications might make them patentable.

4. What is the main purpose of IPR?

a) To provide financial benefits to the government.

b) To provide legal rights to innovators over their creations.

c) To restrict the use of any new inventions.

d) To document traditional knowledge.

5. What is the primary difference between "Bioprospecting" and "Biopiracy"?

a) There is no difference.

b) Bioprospecting is legal, while biopiracy is illegal.

c) Biopiracy involves the study of indigenous knowledge.

d) Bioprospecting refers to the unauthorized use of biological resources.

6. For what purpose is the Nagoya Protocol established?

a) To encourage biopiracy.

b) To document traditional knowledge.

c) For the sharing of benefits from genetic resources.

d) To restrict the use of genetic resources.

7. In the context of the Turmeric case, why was the patent revoked?

a) Because the USPTO favored India.

b) Due to lack of evidence from CSIR.

c) Turmeric's therapeutic properties were part of prior art.

d) The University of Mississippi failed to present their case.

8. The Neem tree is indigenous to which region?

a) Africa

b) Europe

c) North America

d) Indian subcontinent

9. What is the "Myriad Genetics" case related to?

a) DNA sequences

b) Neem tree

c) Turmeric

d) Traditional farming techniques

10. What does the Traditional Knowledge Digital Library (TKDL) primarily aim to do?

a) Provide public access to traditional recipes.

b) Document traditional medicinal knowledge.

c) Grant patents on traditional knowledge.

d) Promote biopiracy.

11. Which of the following is NOT a regulatory requirement for natural products?

a) Identity and Quality

b) Safety

c) Popularity

d) Efficacy

12. In which case was the fungicidal property of a natural product in question?

a) Myriad Genetics

b) Neem case

c) Turmeric case

d) TKDL

13. Which body challenged the patent related to turmeric's use in wound healing?

a) IFOAM

b) EPO

c) CSIR

d) USPTO

14. Which right recognizes the contributions of farmers in conserving plant genetic resources?
   a) IPR
   b) Patent
   c) Farmer's Right
   d) Breeder's Right
15. What is the primary concern with patenting aspects of Traditional Knowledge?
   a) Its commercial potential
   b) Its novelty and prior art
   c) Its widespread availability
   d) Its modern relevance
16. Which international agreement provides a framework for sharing benefits arising from the use of genetic resources?
   a) Kyoto Protocol
   b) Paris Agreement
   c) Nagoya Protocol
   d) Montreal Protocol
17. For a natural product to be patented, it must NOT be:
   a) Useful
   b) Novel
   c) Obvious
   d) Affordable
18. What does the term "Bioprospecting" refer to?
   a) Illegal extraction of biological resources
   b) Exploration of natural sources for commercial applications
   c) Traditional farming techniques
   d) Study of biochemistry in universities

19. Farmers' rights allow them to:

a) Use patented seeds without any restrictions

b) Modify any plant genetically

c) Save, use, exchange, and sell farm-saved seeds

d) Always sell seeds at a higher price

20. Which of the following is a patenting requirement that ensures a patent application provides sufficient details?

a) Novelty

b) Utility

c) Non-obviousness

d) Enablement

Short Answer Type Questions (Subjective)

1. Define "Novelty" in the context of patenting natural products.
2. How does the "Myriad Genetics" case influence the patenting of naturally occurring substances?
3. Explain the significance of the Turmeric patent case.
4. How does the Neem case highlight the importance of traditional knowledge?
5. What is the primary objective of the Traditional Knowledge Digital Library (TKDL)?
6. Describe the difference between "Bioprospecting" and "Biopiracy".
7. What is the importance of "Access and Benefit Sharing (ABS)" in the context of natural products?
8. Explain the "Enablement" requirement for patenting.
9. How do regulatory bodies ensure the consistent quality and identity of natural products?

10. What is the difference between drug and supplement distinction in the context of natural products?
11. Define "Breeder's Right" and its significance.
12. Describe the patenting challenges associated with Traditional Knowledge.
13. What is the "Nagoya Protocol" and why is it significant?
14. Explain the concept of "Nature-derived vs. Naturally Occurring" in patenting.
15. How do the patenting requirements ensure that an invention is not evident to experts in the field?
16. Describe the implications of the Neem patent case.
17. How does the "Non-obviousness/Inventive Step" requirement impact the patentability of natural products?
18. What is the significance of "Good Manufacturing Practices (GMP)" for natural products?
19. Describe the role of the Indian Council of Scientific and Industrial Research (CSIR) in the Turmeric patent case.
20. Explain the importance of "Benefit Sharing" in the context of Traditional Knowledge and Natural Products.

Long Answer Type Questions (Subjective)

1. Discuss in detail the patenting aspects of Traditional Knowledge and Natural Products and their implications on global commerce.
2. Describe the Turmeric patent case, its background, the arguments made, the outcome, and its implications.
3. Elaborate on the Neem patent case, its significance in the discourse of traditional knowledge, and the lessons learned from it.
4. Discuss the importance of documenting and protecting traditional knowledge in the context of global intellectual property rights.

5. Explain the challenges faced by natural products in meeting the patenting requirements and the evolution of these requirements over time.
6. Discuss the ethical considerations surrounding bioprospecting and the commercialization of natural products.
7. Elaborate on the role of regulatory requirements in ensuring the safety, efficacy, and quality of natural products in the market.
8. Discuss the intersection of indigenous rights, commerce, bioprospecting, and intellectual property in the context of natural products and traditional knowledge.
9. Elaborate on the concept of "Access and Benefit Sharing (ABS)" and its significance in international agreements related to genetic resources.
10. Describe the challenges and considerations in patenting natural products derived from traditional knowledge, taking into account cultural sensitivity and the potential for cultural appropriation.

Answer Key for MCQs

1. (b) Exclusive rights to an invention for a specific period.
2. (d) Affordability
3. (d) Modifications or specific applications might make them patentable.
4. (b) To provide legal rights to innovators over their creations.
5. (b) Bioprospecting is legal, while biopiracy is illegal.
6. (c) For the sharing of benefits from genetic resources.
7. (c) Turmeric's therapeutic properties were part of prior art.
8. (d) Indian subcontinent
9. (a) DNA sequences
10. (b) Document traditional medicinal knowledge.
11. (c) Popularity

12.(b) Neem case

13.(c) CSIR

14.(c) Farmer's Right

15.(b) Its novelty and prior art

16.(c) Nagoya Protocol

17.(d) Affordable

18.(b) Exploration of natural sources for commercial applications

19.(c) Save, use, exchange, and sell farm-saved seeds

20.(d) Enablement

CHAPTER - 11

REGULATIONS ISSUE

The Indian pharmaceutical and traditional medicine landscape is governed by a set of regulations, primarily outlined in the Drugs and Cosmetics Act, 1940. Within this context, the role of the Drugs Technical Advisory Board (DTAB) is crucial, especially in shaping the direction and policies for various medicines, including Ayurveda, Siddha, and Unani (ASU) formulations.

DRUGS TECHNICAL ADVISORY BOARD (DTAB) AND ITS RELEVANCE TO ASU MEDICINES:

1. **Composition and Structure:**
   a. DTAB is the highest technical body under the Drugs and Cosmetics Act, 1940. Its composition includes experts from various fields of medicine and pharmaceuticals. Regarding ASU, the Board also includes experts from the fields of Ayurveda, Siddha, and Unani to ensure informed decisions regarding these traditional systems of medicine.
2. **Role and Responsibilities:**
   a. DTAB advises both the Central and State Governments on technical matters arising out of the administration of the Drugs and Cosmetics Act. This includes matters related to the safety, efficacy, and quality of drugs.
   b. It is responsible for giving advice on the matters of drug regulation, making recommendations for changes in the legal framework, and providing guidelines on new regulations.
3. **Involvement in ASU Medicine Regulation:**
   a. While the DTAB is not exclusively for ASU medicines, its considerations include these traditional medicine systems. It deliberates on standards of

ASU medicines, manufacturing practices, quality control, research, and more.

b. Recommendations by DTAB play a significant role in shaping the standards and guidelines that manufacturers and practitioners of ASU medicines need to adhere to.

4. **Updates and Amendments:**
   a. With the ever-evolving landscape of pharmaceuticals and traditional medicines, DTAB continually reviews the Drugs and Cosmetics Act and its rules. In relation to ASU medicines, DTAB might recommend updates or amendments based on new research, global standards, or any reported issues with current practices or formulations.

5. **Collaboration with Other Committees:**
   a. For specific technical matters or to gain a more detailed understanding, DTAB often works in conjunction with specialized committees or sub-committees. This ensures that the board's recommendations and decisions are well-informed and comprehensive.

Importance of DTAB for ASU Medicines:

The traditional medicine systems of Ayurveda, Siddha, and Unani have a rich history in India. With globalization, there's an increasing interest in these traditional formulations worldwide. As such, ensuring the safety, efficacy, and quality of these medicines is of paramount importance. DTAB's role in shaping the regulatory landscape ensures that ASU medicines not only maintain their traditional integrity but also meet modern scientific standards.

The Drugs Consultative Committee (DCC) is another significant regulatory body in the realm of drug regulation in India, functioning under the Drugs and Cosmetics Act, 1940. While it's not exclusive to Ayurveda, Siddha, and Unani

(ASU) medicines, the DCC plays an essential role in addressing issues and challenges faced by these traditional medicine systems.

DRUGS CONSULTATIVE COMMITTEE (DCC) AND ITS RELEVANCE TO ASU MEDICINES:

1. Composition and Structure:
    a. The DCC is made up of representatives from the Central Drugs Standard Control Organization (CDSCO), as well as drug control authorities from Indian states and union territories.
    b. It provides a platform for state and central drug control authorities to share experiences, discuss challenges, and resolve various issues pertaining to the effective implementation of the Drugs and Cosmetics Act.
2. Role and Responsibilities:
    a. The DCC's primary function is to secure uniformity throughout India in the enforcement of the Drugs and Cosmetics Act.
    b. It advises both the Central and State Governments on any other matter treading upon the Drugs and Cosmetics Act.
    c. The DCC discusses challenges in the implementation of the Act and offers solutions to mitigate them.
3. Involvement in ASU Medicine Regulation:
    a. Within the realm of ASU medicines, DCC ensures that the standards and guidelines set out for these traditional systems are uniformly applied across the country. This uniformity ensures that an ASU medicine produced or sold in one part of India meets the same standards as in another part.

b. The DCC addresses challenges faced by the states in the implementation of regulations pertaining to ASU medicines and harmonizes the approaches to overcome these challenges.

4. Meetings and Deliberations:
   a. The DCC meets at regular intervals to discuss various topics related to drug regulations. The issues related to ASU medicines, including challenges faced in manufacturing, quality control, and distribution, often feature in their deliberations.
   b. Resolutions and decisions made in these meetings can have a direct impact on the regulatory landscape for ASU medicines.
5. Collaboration with Other Committees:
   a. The DCC collaborates and consults with other committees and bodies like the Drugs Technical Advisory Board (DTAB) to ensure comprehensive decision-making. This collaboration becomes especially crucial when technical expertise or further insights are required on specific matters.

Importance of DCC for ASU Medicines:

The DCC plays a pivotal role in bringing uniformity in the enforcement of regulations across all Indian states and territories. Given the rich tapestry of traditional medicine practices in India, it's essential to have a central platform where representatives from various regions can discuss, deliberate, and ensure that the quality and standards of ASU medicines are consistent across the board.

For stakeholders in the ASU sector, keeping an eye on the deliberations and decisions of the DCC is vital to understand the evolving regulatory scenario and ensure compliance with the standards set by the committee.

REGULATION OF MANUFACTURE OF ASU DRUGS - SCHEDULE Z OF DRUGS & COSMETICS ACT FOR ASU DRUGS

The regulation of Ayurveda, Siddha, and Unani (ASU) drugs' manufacture in India is governed by the Drugs & Cosmetics Act, 1940, and the rules framed under it. An important section of this regulation is Schedule Z, which specifically pertains to standards to be complied with by manufacturers of ASU medicines.

Regulation of Manufacture of ASU Drugs under Schedule Z:

1. **Scope of Schedule Z:** Schedule Z of the Drugs & Cosmetics Rules lays down the requirements and guidelines for the manufacture of ASU drugs, ensuring that they are produced under conditions that guarantee their safety, efficacy, and quality.
2. **Manufacturing Premises:** The premises where ASU drugs are manufactured must conform to the standards laid down in Schedule Z. The infrastructure should facilitate cleanliness, hygienic conditions, and ensure that cross-contamination does not occur.
3. **Equipment:** The schedule outlines the types of equipment and apparatus that are necessary for the production of ASU drugs. This includes equipment for processes like grinding, sieving, distillation, and more.
4. **Quality Control:** Every manufacturer involved in the production of ASU drugs must maintain a quality control section. This section is tasked with checking raw materials, monitoring manufacturing processes, and conducting tests on finished products to ensure that they meet the prescribed standards.

Quality control (QC) is a critical aspect of the manufacturing process, especially for medicines, including ASU (Ayurveda, Siddha, and Unani) drugs. Ensuring that ASU drugs meet stringent quality standards is essential for patient safety and to guarantee therapeutic efficacy. Here's a deeper dive into the quality control aspects for ASU drug manufacturing:

A. Quality Control Section:

a. **Infrastructure:** The manufacturing facility should have a well-defined QC section equipped with all necessary instruments and equipment to carry out the requisite tests.

b. **Personnel:** It should be staffed by qualified personnel who possess the necessary expertise in ASU drug testing. This team should be able to authenticate, analyze, and certify the quality of raw materials, in-process materials, and finished products.

B. Checking Raw Materials:

a. **Authentication:** Especially in ASU formulations where herbal ingredients are prevalent, correct identification of raw materials is essential. This is done through macroscopic and microscopic examination, phytochemical analysis, and other modern techniques, when necessary.

b. **Purity Tests:** Raw materials should be tested for contaminants, adulterants, and other unwanted substances. This ensures that the starting ingredients are of the highest quality.

C. Monitoring Manufacturing Processes:

a. **In-process Quality Checks:** During the manufacturing process, at various stages, in-process checks are vital. They ensure that the formulation is developing correctly and meets interim quality benchmarks.

b. **Documentation:** All steps in the manufacturing process and their associated QC checks should be thoroughly documented. This provides a traceable record and helps in investigations should there be any quality issues later.

D. Testing Finished Products:

a. **Physical and Chemical Analysis:** Finished products are tested for various physical and chemical attributes. This could include tests for appearance, pH, consistency (for semi-solid preparations), assay of active ingredients, etc.
b. **Microbial Testing:** Finished products are tested for microbial contamination to ensure that they are free from harmful bacteria, fungi, and other pathogens.
c. **Stability Testing:** This ensures that the product will retain its quality, safety, and efficacy throughout its shelf life. It's particularly important for ASU drugs, as many are made from natural ingredients that can degrade over time.
d. **Packaging Inspection:** The QC section also inspects the packaging to ensure it's appropriate for the drug, provides adequate protection, and contains the right information labels.

E. Documentation and Record Keeping:

a. Keeping records of all QC tests is crucial. This helps in traceability, accountability, and in case of audits or reviews.
b. Batch records, test results, calibration records of equipment, and any anomalies or observations should be meticulously documented.

F. Regular Calibration and Maintenance:

a. The equipment used in QC should be regularly calibrated to ensure that they provide accurate and reliable results.
b. Scheduled maintenance is necessary to keep the instruments in optimal working condition.

G. Feedback Loop:

a. Quality control is not just about identifying problems but also about rectifying them. Feedback from the QC section should be integrated into the manufacturing process to make necessary adjustments and improvements.

H. Regulatory Adherence:

a. The QC section should be aware of and adhere to the latest regulatory guidelines. Periodic training might be necessary to ensure the team is updated with any changes in the regulatory landscape.

5. **Raw Material:** The quality of raw materials is crucial for ASU medicines. The schedule ensures that raw materials, especially herbs and minerals, are authenticated, and their quality is maintained.
6. **Storage Conditions:** Schedule Z provides guidelines for proper storage conditions to ensure the potency, efficacy, and stability of ASU drugs. storage conditions play an integral role in ensuring that the potency, efficacy, and stability of ASU (Ayurveda, Siddha, and Unani) drugs are maintained. Improper storage conditions can lead to the degradation of the drug, making it ineffective or, in worse cases, harmful.

Storage Conditions as per Schedule Z for ASU Drugs:

1. **Temperature Control:**
   a. Many ASU drugs have specific temperature requirements to maintain their efficacy. Some might need to be stored in a cool place, while others may require refrigeration.
   b. Avoiding exposure to excessive heat is often stressed, as it can destabilize many formulations, especially those containing volatile components.
2. **Humidity Control:**
   a. Moisture can be detrimental to many ASU formulations, especially powders and herbs.

b. The storage area should be free from dampness to avoid the growth of fungi or other microbes.

3. **Light-sensitive Drugs:**
   a. Some ingredients in ASU drugs might be sensitive to light, leading to their degradation or reduced potency.
   b. Such drugs should be stored in dark containers or in areas shielded from direct sunlight.
4. **Aeration and Ventilation:**
   a. Proper ventilation ensures that the storage area remains free from mold and microbial growth, especially in regions with high humidity.
   b. Moreover, certain ASU preparations, like some oils, might need aeration.
5. **Segregation:**
   a. Different drugs or raw materials should be stored separately to prevent cross-contamination.
   b. Potentially toxic or reactive substances should be stored with particular care and adequately labeled.
6. **Container and Packaging:**
   a. The type of container can influence the drug's stability. While some drugs are best stored in glass bottles, others might require plastic, metal, or other packaging materials.
   b. The containers should be airtight to prevent the ingress of moisture and contaminants.
7. **Protection from Pests:**
   a. The storage area should be free from pests like rodents or insects. Many raw materials, especially herbs, can be susceptible to pest infestations.
8. **Shelf Life:**

a. ASU drugs should be used within their prescribed shelf life, which should be clearly indicated on their labels.
b. Older stock should be used first to ensure that drugs do not exceed their shelf life while in storage.

9. Special Storage Instructions:

a. Some ASU drugs might have specific storage instructions due to their unique composition or sensitivity. Manufacturers should clearly mention these on the packaging.

10.Security:

a. The storage area should be secure to prevent unauthorized access, contamination, or tampering.

11.**Personnel:**

a. Manufacturers must employ competent technical staff with relevant qualifications to oversee and manage the production of ASU drugs. This includes personnel for manufacturing, quality control, and traditional medicine experts to authenticate the traditional formulations.

12.Documentation and Records:

a. Proper records need to be maintained for various processes, including raw material procurement, manufacturing, quality control tests, and distribution. The schedule specifies the types of records and the duration for which they need to be retained.

13.Licensing:

a. Before a manufacturer can produce ASU drugs, they must obtain a license. The licensing procedure ensures that the manufacturer meets all the requirements laid down in Schedule Z and is competent to produce ASU drugs that are safe, effective, and of high quality.

14.Inspections:

a. Regulatory authorities conduct inspections of manufacturing premises to ensure adherence to the conditions and standards laid out in Schedule Z.

15. Labelling and Packaging:

a. ASU drug packaging and labeling must provide adequate information about the drug and ensure its safe use. Schedule Z dictates specific details that should be present on the label.

Importance of Schedule Z:

Regulating the manufacture of ASU drugs is crucial to protect public health and maintain the trust in traditional systems of medicine. Schedule Z of the Drugs & Cosmetics Rules ensures that ASU drugs are manufactured under stringent conditions, making them safe and effective for consumption.

For manufacturers and stakeholders in the ASU sector, understanding and complying with the guidelines and standards laid down in Schedule Z is essential. Not only does it ensure legal compliance, but it also guarantees that the ASU drugs produced are of the highest quality.

MCQs (Objective)

1. What is the primary body governing the technical aspects of the Drugs and Cosmetics Act, 1940?

   a) Drugs Consultative Committee (DCC)

   b) Central Drugs Standard Control Organization (CDSCO)

   c) Drugs Technical Advisory Board (DTAB)

   d) Ayurveda, Siddha, and Unani (ASU) Board

2. Which of the following is NOT a responsibility of the DTAB?

   a) Advising on the administration of the Drugs and Cosmetics Act.

   b) Establishing global trade policies.

   c) Recommending changes in the legal framework.

d) Providing guidelines on new regulations.

3. Which committee ensures uniformity in the enforcement of the Drugs and Cosmetics Act throughout India?

   a) DTAB

   b) DCC

   c) CDSCO

   d) ASU Committee

4. What is the primary focus of Schedule Z in the Drugs & Cosmetics Rules?

   a) International trade regulations.

   b) Requirements for the manufacture of ASU drugs.

   c) Guidelines for modern pharmaceuticals.

   d) Licensing procedures for drug sales.

5. Which of the following is NOT a quality control check for ASU drugs?

   a) Physical and Chemical Analysis

   b) Temperature regulation during storage

   c) Microbial Testing

   d) Light sensitivity test

6. Before manufacturing ASU drugs, what is essential for a manufacturer to obtain?

   a) International approval

   b) Approval from traditional healers

   c) A license

   d) A pharmaceutical degree

7. Which committee collaborates with specialized sub-committees for specific technical matters?

   a) DCC

   b) CDSCO

c) DTAB

d) ASU Committee

8. What is the primary role of the DCC?

a) To provide technical guidelines

b) To secure uniformity in enforcing the Drugs and Cosmetics Act across India

c) To manage international relations

d) To license ASU practitioners

9. Which body has representatives from the Central Drugs Standard Control Organization (CDSCO)?

a) DTAB

b) ASU Board

c) DCC

d) Quality Control Committee

10. Which of the following is an aspect of storage conditions as per Schedule Z for ASU Drugs? a) Light-sensitive drug storage

b) Temperature variations for testing drug stability

c) Drug flavor preservation

d) Color preservation in drugs

11. Whose responsibility is it to ensure that a drug produced in one part of India meets the same standards as in another part?

a) DTAB

b) ASU Committee

c) DCC

d) CDSCO

12. What does Schedule Z emphasize regarding the manufacturing premises of ASU drugs?

a) It should be located centrally.

b) It should be vast.

c) It should facilitate cleanliness and prevent cross-contamination.

d) It should be aesthetically pleasing

13. What is essential for equipment used in Quality Control?

a) They should be modern.

b) They should be regularly calibrated.

c) They should be imported.

d) They should be automated.

14. In the context of ASU drug manufacturing, why is documentation important?

a) For marketing purposes.

b) For international trade.

c) For traceability and accountability.

d) For aesthetic reasons.

15. Which of the following is NOT a part of the Quality Control process for ASU drugs?

a) Feedback Loop

b) Temperature regulation during storage

c) Regular Calibration and Maintenance

d) Monitoring Manufacturing Processes

16. Which body specifically lays down requirements for ASU drug manufacturing?

a) DCC

b) Schedule Z

c) CDSCO

d) DTAB

17. Which committee plays a role in ensuring the safety, efficacy, and quality of ASU medicines for global interest?

a) DCC

b) DTAB

c) ASU Board

d) CDSCO

18. Why is proper ventilation crucial in the storage area for ASU drugs?

a) To provide aeration for certain ASU preparations.

b) To maintain a certain temperature.

c) To enhance the aroma of the drugs.

d) To ensure a pleasant working environment.

19. What should be clearly indicated on the labels of ASU drugs regarding storage?

a) Manufacturing date

b) International certifications

c) Shelf life

d) Price

20. The Drugs and Cosmetics Act, 1940, primarily regulates which of the following in India?

a) Export of pharmaceuticals

b) International collaborations

c) Manufacturing and distribution of drugs and cosmetics

d) Pricing of medicines

Short Answer Type Questions (Subjective)

1. What is the role of the Drugs Technical Advisory Board (DTAB) in the context of the Drugs and Cosmetics Act, 1940?
2. Describe the significance of the Drugs Consultative Committee (DCC) in ensuring uniformity across India.
3. How does Schedule Z impact the manufacturing of ASU drugs?

4. Explain the importance of Quality Control in the manufacturing process of ASU drugs.
5. Why is the proper storage of ASU drugs crucial?
6. How does the DCC ensure the uniform application of ASU medicine standards across India?
7. Describe the significance of the labeling and packaging of ASU drugs as per Schedule Z.
8. What is the relevance of the DTAB in shaping the regulatory landscape for ASU medicines?
9. How does the DCC facilitate communication between state and central drug control authorities?
10. Why is it important to have experts from Ayurveda, Siddha, and Unani on the DTAB?
11. Describe the role of Quality Control in ensuring the efficacy of ASU drugs.
12. How does Schedule Z ensure the safety and efficacy of ASU medicines?
13. What is the significance of regular calibration and maintenance in the Quality Control process?
14. How does the DCC address challenges in the implementation of ASU medicine regulations?
15. Why is documentation and record-keeping crucial in the ASU drug manufacturing process?
16. Explain the importance of temperature control in the storage of ASU drugs.
17. Describe the significance of the feedback loop in Quality Control.
18. How do the DTAB and DCC collaborate in the realm of drug regulation?
19. Why is the authentication of raw materials essential in ASU drug manufacturing?

20. Explain the importance of stability testing in the Quality Control process for ASU drugs.

Long Answer Type Questions (Subjective)

1. Discuss in detail the role and responsibilities of the Drugs Technical Advisory Board (DTAB) and its impact on ASU medicines.
2. Elaborate on the significance of the Drugs Consultative Committee (DCC) in ensuring uniformity in the enforcement of the Drugs and Cosmetics Act across India.
3. Describe the various aspects of Quality Control in the manufacturing of ASU drugs and their importance in ensuring safety and efficacy.
4. Discuss the guidelines and standards laid down in Schedule Z for the manufacturing of ASU drugs.
5. Explain the challenges faced in the storage of ASU drugs and the guidelines provided by Schedule Z to address these challenges.
6. Elaborate on the importance of the collaboration between the DTAB and specialized sub-committees in shaping the regulatory landscape for ASU medicines.
7. Discuss the significance of proper documentation and record-keeping in the ASU drug manufacturing process and its role in ensuring quality and safety.
8. Describe the role of the DCC in addressing challenges and harmonizing approaches related to ASU medicines across different states in India.
9. Elaborate on the significance of the licensing procedure for manufacturers of ASU drugs and the standards they must meet as per Schedule Z.
10. Discuss the importance of the DTAB and DCC in preserving the traditional integrity of ASU medicines while ensuring they meet modern scientific standards.

Answer Key for MCQs

1. (c) Drugs Technical Advisory Board (DTAB)
2. (b) Establishing global trade policies.
3. (b) DCC
4. (b) Requirements for the manufacture of ASU drugs.
5. (b) Temperature regulation during storage
6. (c) A license
7. (c) DTAB
8. (b) To secure uniformity in enforcing the Drugs and Cosmetics Act across India
9. (c) DCC
10. (a) Light-sensitive drug storage
11. (c) DCC
12. (c) It should facilitate cleanliness and prevent cross-contamination.
13. (b) They should be regularly calibrated.
14. (c) For traceability and accountability.
15. (b) Temperature regulation during storage
16. (b) Schedule Z
17. (b) DTAB
18. (a) To provide aeration for certain ASU preparations.
19. (c) Shelf life
20. (c) Manufacturing and distribution of drugs and cosmetics.

CHAPTER - 12

GENERAL INTRODUCTION TO HERBAL INDUSTRY

HERBAL DRUGS INDUSTRY: PRESENT SCOPE AND FUTURE PROSPECTS

Present Scope:

1. **Global Reach:** The herbal drugs industry, often interlinked with traditional medicine, has gained significant attention worldwide. In many countries, especially in Asia, Africa, and Latin America, a large proportion of the population relies on herbal medicines for their primary healthcare.
2. **Consumer Awareness:** With an increasing number of consumers becoming health-conscious and seeking natural remedies, there's a surge in demand for herbal products.
3. **Research and Development:** Modern scientific methods are now being employed to validate the therapeutic benefits of various herbal formulations. Many established pharmaceutical companies are investing in R&D of herbal drugs.
4. **Standardization and Quality Control:** To ensure efficacy and safety, standardization of herbal extracts and products is becoming more prevalent. Modern analytical techniques are applied to assess the quality of herbal products.
5. **Integrative Medicine:** Many health practitioners are adopting a holistic approach, integrating herbal drugs with conventional medicine to provide comprehensive treatment solutions.

6. **Regulation:** Governments in various countries are increasingly recognizing the importance of regulating the herbal drugs industry. This includes setting standards for cultivation, harvesting, production, and marketing of herbal drugs.

Future Prospects:

1. **Market Growth:** The global herbal drugs market is expected to witness substantial growth, driven by the increasing consumer preference for natural products and the potential health benefits they offer.
2. **Phytopharmaceutical Development:** With modern scientific tools, it's expected that new phytopharmaceuticals (medicines derived from plants) will be developed. These drugs will undergo rigorous testing and standardization similar to conventional pharmaceuticals.
3. **Biotechnological Advancements**: Biotechnology might play a crucial role in enhancing the quality and yield of medicinal plants. Genetic engineering and plant tissue culture can lead to consistent and enhanced production of therapeutic phytochemicals.
4. **Nanotechnology:** The application of nanotechnology in the herbal drugs industry can improve the delivery systems of herbal formulations, enhancing their bioavailability and therapeutic efficacy.
5. **Eco-friendly Cultivation:** Sustainable cultivation practices will be more widely adopted to ensure the conservation of medicinal plants and biodiversity.
6. **Global Collaborations:** International collaborations can help in the sharing of traditional medicinal knowledge, standardized research methodologies, and regulatory practices.
7. **Customized Herbal Formulations:** With the growth in personalized medicine, there might be a trend towards developing herbal formulations tailored to individual genetic and health profiles.

Challenges:

While the future seems promising, the herbal drugs industry faces challenges:

1. **Standardization Issues:** Unlike synthetic drugs, herbal drugs consist of complex mixtures, making standardization challenging.
2. **Overharvesting:** Some medicinal plants are endangered due to overharvesting and habitat destruction.
3. **Safety Concerns:** Not all herbal drugs are safe. They can interact with other drugs or have side effects.
4. **Regulatory Hurdles:** Different countries have different regulatory standards for herbal products, making international commerce complex.

A BRIEF ACCOUNT OF PLANT BASED INDUSTRIES AND INSTITUTIONS INVOLVED IN WORK ON MEDICINAL AND AROMATIC PLANTS IN INDIA

India has a rich heritage of using medicinal and aromatic plants (MAPs) that is deeply rooted in its traditional systems of medicine like Ayurveda, Siddha, and Unani. Given this backdrop, several industries and institutions are dedicated to the study, cultivation, and marketing of these plants in the country. Here's a brief account of plant-based industries and prominent institutions involved with MAPs in India:

Plant-Based Industries in India:

1. **Ayurvedic Pharmaceutical Companies:** Companies like Dabur, Himalaya Drug Company, Baidyanath, and Patanjali Ayurved are among the major players in the market that produce a range of products, from personal care to therapeutic medicines, based on herbal formulations.

2. **Essential Oils and Aromatic Product Manufacturers:** The cultivation of aromatic plants like rose, jasmine, lemongrass, and vetiver has led to the rise of industries producing essential oils, perfumes, and aromatic products for domestic and export markets.
3. **Herbal Cosmetic Industries:** Brands like Forest Essentials, Biotique, and VLCC have carved a niche for themselves in the herbal cosmetics market.
4. **Exporters:** India is a significant exporter of medicinal herbs and aromatic plants, with several companies dedicated solely to the export of these raw materials and products to global markets.

Institutions Involved in Work on MAPs in India:

1. **Central Institute of Medicinal and Aromatic Plants (CIMAP):** Located in Lucknow, CIMAP is a premier institution under the Council of Scientific & Industrial Research (CSIR). It focuses on the research and development of medicinal and aromatic plants, catering to the needs of the agriculture, pharmaceutical, and fragrance industries.
2. **National Medicinal Plants Board (NMPB):** Set up by the Government of India, its main objective is the promotion, cultivation, conservation, and proper dissemination of knowledge about medicinal plants
3. **Ayurvedic Universities and Colleges:** Several universities, such as Gujarat Ayurveda University, National Institute of Ayurveda, and Banaras Hindu University, offer courses on Ayurveda and conduct research on medicinal plants.
4. **Agharkar Research Institute (ARI):** Located in Pune, ARI conducts research on plant sciences, including medicinal plants.

5. **Tropical Botanic Garden and Research Institute (TBGRI)**: Located in Kerala, TBGRI's activities are centered around the conservation and sustainable utilization of the tropical plant diversity, especially the rich array of medicinal plants in the Western Ghats region.
6. **FRLHT (Foundation for Revitalisation of Local Health Traditions)**: Based in Bengaluru, it's focused on the conservation and sustainable use of medicinal plants, integrating traditional knowledge with modern science.
7. **State Forest Departments and Agricultural Universities:** They conduct research, offer training, and implement programs for the cultivation and conservation of medicinal and aromatic plants.

SCHEDULE T - GMP

Schedule T delineates the Good Manufacturing Practices (GMP) for the preparation of Ayurvedic, Siddha, and Unani (ASU) medicines in India. It's an integral part of the Drugs and Cosmetics Act 1940 and its Rules 1945. GMP aims to ensure the safety, efficacy, and quality of medicines by emphasizing standardization in manufacturing processes.

Objectives of Schedule T - GMP:

1. **Quality Assurance:** To ensure that the medicines are consistently produced and controlled to the quality standards appropriate for their intended use and as required by the marketing authorization.
2. **Safety:** To ensure that the products are safe for human consumption and devoid of contamination.
3. **Standardization and Uniformity:** To guarantee that the products are consistent in terms of quality and performance, batch after batch.
4. **Scientific Approach:** To advocate a systematic and scientifically sound approach to all aspects of the manufacturing process.

Components of GMP (Schedule – T):

1. **Factory Premises:** It includes details about location & surroundings, buildings & construction, water supply, disposal of water & waste, sanitation, medical services, and other utilities
2. **Warehousing:** Guidelines are provided for raw material stores, packaging material stores, finished goods stores, rejected goods stores, machinery and equipment stores, quarantine storage, and records.
3. **Manufacturing Area:** Requirements for the various sections like powder, tablet, capsule, avaleha (a thick liquid or semi-solid preparation), asava/arista (fermented medicines), churna (powdered herbal mix), etc.
4. **Equipment**: Guidelines for equipment selection, use, cleaning, and maintenance.
5. **Raw Materials:** Emphasis on the use of genuine, authenticated, and non-contaminated raw materials. Also, guidelines for collection, storage, and use.
6. **Production:** Procedures and precautions, in-process quality checks, time cycles of production, sanitary and hygienic requirements, and standardization & quality control of finished products.
7. **Quality Control:** Instructions for the maintenance of a quality control department, instruments, and equipment, testing of raw materials, and finished products.
8. **Documentation and Records:** Maintenance of records for raw material, production, quality control, distribution, staff training, and any issues or recalls.
9. **Quality Assurance:** Parameters for in-process and finished product quality checks.
10. **Personnel:** Requirements for the hygiene, health, and training of personnel. Recommendations for avoiding contamination from personnel.

11. **Sanitation and Hygiene:** Guidelines to ensure cleanliness within the manufacturing unit and its surroundings. Instructions for regular cleaning, pest control, and personnel hygiene.
12. **Recall and Complaint Handling:** Procedures to handle complaints and recalls efficiently, ensuring patient safety.
13. **Self-assessment/Audit:** Recommendations for regular self-audits to ensure compliance with GMP guidelines.

Infrastructural Requirements as per Schedule -T:

1. **Factory Building & Premises:**
   a. The design and construction of the factory building should be appropriate for producing the intended categories of drugs.
   b. It should prevent the entry of dust, dirt, and other contaminants. It should also deter the entry of rodents, insects, and birds.
   c. The production area should be clearly demarcated from other areas to avoid cross-contamination.
2. **Location:**
   a. The manufacturing unit should ideally be located away from industries that discharge fumes, smoke, dust, and other pollutants to avoid contamination.
   b. It should be in an environment that's conducive for the manufacture of medicinal products without risk of contamination.
3. **Layout & Design:**
   a. The layout should be such that there is a logical sequence of operations to prevent cross-contamination.

b. Separate areas should be designated for different activities, like the reception of raw materials, storage, processing, manufacturing, packaging, quarantine, and dispatch.

4. **Water Supply:**
   a. There should be an ample supply of clean and potable water. If the water needs treatment (like deionization or purification), the necessary facilities should be provided.
   b. Regular testing of water used in the manufacturing process should be conducted to ensure its potability and appropriateness for use.
5. **Internal Infrastructure:**
   a. Walls: Should be smooth, free from cracks, and painted with a durable, washable paint. This aids in easy cleaning and reduces dust accumulation.
   b. Floors: Should be made of an impervious material, ensuring they're easy to clean and don't absorb or retain substances.
   c. Ceilings: Should be designed to prevent the accumulation of dust and to reduce the shedding or flaking of particles.
   d. Windows: Should be fitted with insect screens and made in a way to reduce the accumulation of dust. They should also be easy to clean.
6. **Lighting & Ventilation:**
   a. Adequate natural and/or artificial lighting should be provided.
   b. Effective ventilation systems, possibly with air control facilities (like air heaters or air conditioners), should be in place. Air filtration systems can also be installed to further ensure cleanliness.
   c. Exhaust systems should be designed to minimize cross-contamination.
7. Waste Disposal:

a. Proper facilities should be available for the treatment and disposal of sewage, refuse, and other wastes. These facilities should meet the environmental standards set by regulatory authorities.
b. There should be provisions for the safe and efficient disposal of waste materials like solvents and other contaminants.

WORKING SPACE REQUIREMENTS AS PER SCHEDULE- T:

1. **Adequate Space:** The manufacturing area should have adequate space for the free movement of workers and materials to avoid any mix-up, confusion, and contamination. This also ensures the orderly placement of equipment and materials.
2. **Logical Flow:** The working space should be designed such that there's a logical sequence of operations to ensure the flow of materials and personnel prevents any cross-contamination.
3. **Separate Areas:** Separate, defined areas should be allocated for different operations to avoid contamination. This includes areas for:
   a. Raw material processing
   b. Manufacturing
   c. Packaging
   d. Quality control
   e. Storage of in-process materials
4. **Controlled Environment:** Where necessary, especially in areas where sensitive processes take place or where the product is exposed, environmental conditions like temperature and humidity should be controlled and monitored.

5. **Cleanliness:** The production areas should be kept clean and free from accumulated waste, dust, and other contaminants. There should be regular schedules for cleaning.
6. **Prevention of Cross-Contamination:** If the facility produces multiple products, it should ensure that there's no cross-contamination. This can be achieved through proper design, use of separate equipment or thorough cleaning of equipment between batches, and ensuring personnel don't move between different areas without taking the necessary precautions.
7. **Walls, Floors, and Ceilings:** The design should facilitate cleaning and reduce dust accumulation:
   a. **Walls:** Should be smooth, free from cracks, and easily cleanable.
   b. **Floors:** Should be even, made of impervious materials, and facilitate effective cleaning.
   c. **Ceilings:** Designed to prevent the accumulation of dust and to minimize the shedding or flaking of particles.
8. **Lighting:** Adequate lighting should be provided to enable all operations, including cleaning, to be carried out effectively and safely.
9. **Protection Against Entry:** The working space should be designed in a manner that prevents the entry of pests, dust, and other contaminants. This includes fitting windows and other openings with protective measures like insect screens.

Storage Area Requirements as per Schedule T:

1. **Delineation of Areas:**
   a. Separate areas should be designated for the storage of raw materials, packaging materials, in-process materials, and finished products to prevent any mix-up or contamination.

b. Quarantine areas should be available for materials awaiting quality control clearance.
c. There should be a specified area for rejected materials or products.

2. **Conditions and Environment:**
   a. The storage area should provide protection against climatic conditions like excessive temperature and humidity, as they can impact the quality of the medicines.
   b. Controlled environments might be necessary for some products or materials that are sensitive to light, moisture, or temperature.
3. **Organization:**
   a. Stored materials should be systematically organized, possibly using a First-Expire-First-Out (FEFO) or First-In-First-Out (FIFO) system, to ensure that no outdated materials are used in manufacturing.
   b. Adequate space should be maintained between stored items to allow for easy inspection, cleaning, and pest control activities.
4. **Hygiene and Cleanliness:**
   a. Storage areas should be kept clean and free from accumulated waste, dust, pests, and other contaminants.
   b. Regular cleaning schedules should be maintained.
5. **Protection from Pests:**
   a. Effective measures should be in place to prevent the entry and breeding of pests, rodents, and birds. This might include routine pest control treatments.
6. **Security:**
   a. Storage areas should be secure to prevent unauthorized access. This is vital to avoid tampering, theft, and other security risks.
   b. There should be provisions in place for the proper and safe storage of hazardous materials, if any.

7. **Documentation and Labeling:**
    a. Every stored material should be appropriately labeled, indicating its name, batch number, date of receipt, expiry date, and other relevant details.
    b. Records should be maintained for the receipt and issue of all materials to ensure traceability.
8. **Handling and Movement:**
    a. There should be provisions for the proper handling and movement of materials to prevent breakage, spillage, and other damages.
    b. Equipment like pallets, trolleys, or forklifts can be used to ensure smooth and safe movement.
9. **Rejected and Returned Goods:**
    a. Rejected raw materials and returned finished products should be stored separately from other materials and products to prevent mix-ups.

"Schedule T" of the Drugs and Cosmetics Act, 1940 and its Rules, 1945 outlines the Good Manufacturing Practices (GMP) for Ayurvedic, Siddha, and Unani medicines in India. Proper machinery and equipment, as well as robust standard operating procedures (SOPs), are fundamental to ensuring product quality, safety, and efficacy.

Machinery and Equipment's Requirements as per Schedule T:

1. **Design and Construction:** Machinery and equipment should be designed and constructed so that they can be easily cleaned, maintained, and operated without contamination of the products.
2. **Material:** They should be made of non-reactive, non-absorbent, and corrosion-resistant material.

3. **Placement**: Equipment should be located in a manner that it facilitates its operation and cleaning and doesn't hinder the proper placement, movement, or storage of other equipment or materials.
4. **Maintenance and Calibration:** Machinery and equipment should be routinely maintained and calibrated. Records of maintenance and calibration should be kept.
5. **Cleaning:** Equipment should be cleaned according to defined procedures to prevent contamination. The cleaning procedures and frequency should be documented.
6. **Identification:** Each equipment should be labeled with a distinctive ID or code for identification purposes.
7. **Protection:** Equipment should be designed to minimize any risk of a product mix-up during operation. Protection mechanisms should be in place for machinery with moving parts.

Standard Operating Procedures (SOPs) Requirements as per Schedule T:

1. **Documentation:** SOPs should be documented for all operations that might affect the quality of the product. This includes procedures for receipt and storage of raw materials, production, packaging, quality control, maintenance, and more.
2. **Accessibility:** SOPs should be readily available to the personnel in the respective areas where the operations are being conducted.
3. Content: The SOPs should provide step-by-step, clear, and unambiguous instructions. They should be detailed enough to ensure uniformity in performance and avoid errors.

4. **Training:** Personnel should be trained on the SOPs, and their understanding should be assessed. Training records should be maintained.
5. **Review and Updates:** SOPs should be periodically reviewed and updated whenever necessary to reflect current practices. Changes should be documented, and older versions should be archived.
6. **Approval:** All SOPs should be approved by the designated authority before implementation.
7. **SOPs for Equipment:** These should cover operations like starting and stopping the equipment, cleaning, maintenance, and what to do in case of malfunctions or breakdowns.
8. **Archiving:** Old versions of SOPs should be retained for a specific period, as per regulatory guidelines.

"Schedule T" of the Drugs and Cosmetics Act, 1940 and its Rules, 1945, details the Good Manufacturing Practices (GMP) for Ayurvedic, Siddha, and Unani medicines in India. Health and hygiene of the personnel working in manufacturing areas are vital components of GMP, ensuring that product quality and safety are not compromised.

Health and Hygiene Requirements as per Schedule T:

1. **Personnel Health:**
   a. Workers employed in the manufacturing areas should be free from any contagious or communicable diseases. Periodic medical examinations should be conducted to ensure the health of the employees.
   b. Any person showing signs of illness should not be allowed to work in production areas until fully recovered.
2. **Personal Hygiene:**

a. Personnel should maintain a high degree of personal cleanliness. This includes regular washing of hands, especially after breaks.
b. Hair should be covered, and beards, if any, should also be covered to prevent product contamination.

3. **Clothing:**
   a. Staff working in manufacturing areas should wear clean, appropriate protective clothing that doesn't shed lint or fibers. Such clothing might include uniforms, headcovers, masks, gloves, and footwear, depending on the specific tasks and cleanliness requirements.
   b. Outer clothing or street clothes should not be worn inside production areas.
4. **Training:**
   a. Personnel should be trained in personal hygiene practices relevant to their roles. They should be made aware of the potential risks of contamination from themselves or their surroundings.
   b. Regular refresher training sessions should be conducted to reinforce best practices.
5. **Behaviors:**
   a. Eating, drinking, smoking, or any such activities should not be permitted in production areas. Designated areas should be provided for breaks and meals.
   b. Personal items, cosmetics, or any non-essential items should not be taken into production areas.
6. **Injuries:**
   a. Open cuts, wounds, or injuries should be properly covered with waterproof dressings before an employee can work in areas where products or raw materials are exposed.
7. **Access Restrictions:**

a. Only authorized and trained personnel should be allowed to enter the manufacturing areas. Visitors or non-essential staff should be provided with protective clothing if they need to enter, and they should be accompanied by trained staff.

8. **Restrooms and Facilities:**

    a. Restrooms and changing rooms should be separate from production areas and should be designed to prevent any contamination of the production environment. They should be kept clean and maintained regularly.

In the realm of Good Manufacturing Practices (GMP), particularly as detailed under "Schedule T" of the Drugs and Cosmetics Act, 1940 and its Rules, 1945, for Ayurvedic, Siddha, and Unani medicines in India, documentation and record-keeping play a pivotal role. Proper documentation ensures that processes are consistent and can be audited, while records provide evidence that these processes have been followed.

Documentation and Records Requirements as per Schedule T:

1. **Master Formula Records:**

These provide the blueprint for the production of each product. The record includes details such as the name of the product, ingredients and their quantities, a description of the procedure, packing details, and any special precautions to be followed.

2. **Batch Manufacturing Records:**

Detailed records for each batch of product manufactured. This ensures that each batch has been prepared and controlled in accordance with the master formula.

3. **Standard Operating Procedures (SOPs):**

SOPs are documented procedures that provide step-by-step instructions on how t perform various tasks. SOPs are crucial for maintaining consistency across processes.

4. Logbooks:

These are often maintained for equipment and instruments. They contain records of cleaning, maintenance, calibration, and usage.

5. Quality Control Records:

These detail the testing and quality checks carried out on raw materials, in-process materials, and finished products.

6. Training Records:

Documentation of training sessions, topics covered, attendees, and their assessments should be maintained.

7. Distribution Records:

These detail the batch numbers of products distributed to particular distributors or customers, aiding in traceability.

8. Retention of Records:

All records should be retained for a specific period, as defined by regulatory guidelines. Typically, this is for at least one year after the expiration date of the batch.

9. Archiving:

Outdated documents should be archived but retained to provide a history of changes and decisions.

10. Validation and Calibration Records:

Documentation of the validation of processes and the calibration of equipment ensures that both are functioning as intended and are providing accurate and consistent results.

11.Review and Approval:

All documents should be reviewed for accuracy and completeness by a competent authority. Any changes to documents should be approved by the same or another relevant authority.

12.Security and Access:

Important documents and records should be stored securely to prevent unauthorized access, alterations, or loss. This could be physical security for paper documents or digital security measures for electronic records.

13.Audit Trails:

For electronic records, systems should maintain a secure and retrievable record of all changes, detailing what was changed, by whom, and when.

14.Incident and Deviation Reports:

Any deviations from standard procedures or unexpected incidents should be documented, investigated, and addressed to prevent recurrence.

Multiple choice Questions (MCQs):

1. Which region has seen a significant reliance on herbal medicines for primary healthcare?
   a) North America
   b) Europe
   c) Asia, Africa, and Latin America
   d) Australia

2. Modern scientific methods are being employed to validate the therapeutic benefits of which products?
   a) Synthetic drugs
   b) Genetically modified organisms
   c) Herbal formulations
   d) Cosmetics
3. What is becoming more prevalent to ensure the safety and efficacy of herbal products?
   a) Packaging
   b) Marketing strategies
   c) Standardization and Quality Control
   d) Global distribution
4. What is expected to drive the substantial growth of the global herbal drugs market in the future?
   a) Decreased consumer interest
   b) Rising production costs
   c) Increasing consumer preference for natural products
   d) Government restrictions
5. Biotechnological advancements in the herbal drug industry might lead to:
   a) Reduced importance of medicinal plants
   b) Enhanced production of therapeutic phytochemicals
   c) Reduced research in traditional medicine
   d) Lowered investment in R&D
6. What is a major challenge in the standardization of herbal drugs?
   a) They are easy to produce
   b) They consist of simple mixtures
   c) They consist of complex mixtures

d) They are too expensive

7. Which company is NOT a major player in the Ayurvedic pharmaceutical market in India?
   a) Dabur
   b) Johnson & Johnson
   c) Himalaya Drug Company
   d) Patanjali Ayurved
8. Which institution is primarily focused on research and development of medicinal and aromatic plants?
   a) National Medicinal Plants Board
   b) Central Institute of Medicinal and Aromatic Plants
   c) Banaras Hindu University
   d) Agharkar Research Institute
9. Schedule T of the Drugs and Cosmetics Act, 1940 deals with:
   a) Pricing of drugs
   b) International trade regulations
   c) Good Manufacturing Practices for ASU medicines
   d) Licensing procedures for drug sales
10. Which component is NOT part of the Good Manufacturing Practices (GMP) as per Schedule T?
    a) Factory Premises
    b) Marketing strategies
    c) Quality Control
    d) Equipment
11. What is the primary purpose of Master Formula Records?
    a) To market the product
    b) To provide a blueprint for the production of each product

c) To record employee details

d) To handle complaints

12. According to Schedule T, workers employed in manufacturing areas should be free from:

a) Higher education

b) Contagious diseases

c) Training sessions

d) Modern equipment

13. Equipment used in the manufacturing of ASU medicines should be:

a) Made of absorbent material

b) Made of reactive material

c) Made of corrosion-resistant material

d) Difficult to clean

14. Which of the following is an essential requirement for personnel working in the manufacturing areas as per Schedule T?

a) They should wear street clothes

b) They should eat and drink in the production areas

c) They should maintain a high degree of personal cleanliness

d) They should have open cuts and wounds

15. What does the global reach of the herbal drugs industry primarily indicate?

a) Decline in traditional medicine

b) Significant attention worldwide

c) Limited to specific regions

d) Popularity only in western countries

16. Who should approve all SOPs before implementation?

a) All employees

b) General public

c) Designated authority

d) International agencies

17. What is the primary focus of documentation and records as per Schedule T?

a) Marketing the products

b) Ensuring processes are consistent and can be audited

c) For international trade

d) For aesthetic purposes

18. Which technology is expected to improve the delivery systems of herbal formulations in the future?

a) Biotechnology

b) Information Technology

c) Nanotechnology

d) Rocket Science

19. Sustainable cultivation practices in the future prospects of the herbal drugs industry will ensure:

a) Increased profits

b) Conservation of medicinal plants and biodiversity

c) Increased consumer demands

d) Enhanced global reach

20. In which state is the Tropical Botanic Garden and Research Institute located?

a) Tamil Nadu

b) Uttar Pradesh

c) Kerala

d) Maharashtra

Short Answer Type Questions (Subjective)

1. How has consumer awareness impacted the herbal drugs industry?

2. What role does research and development play in the herbal drugs industry?
3. Explain the significance of integrative medicine in the context of herbal drugs.
4. How does biotechnological advancement promise to enhance the herbal drugs industry?
5. Describe the importance of eco-friendly cultivation in the future prospects of herbal drugs.
6. What challenges does the herbal drugs industry face regarding standardization?
7. Briefly explain the role of the National Medicinal Plants Board in India.
8. What is the importance of the "Factory Building & Premises" component in Schedule T's GMP?
9. Why is the calibration of machinery and equipment crucial in ASU medicine manufacturing?
10. Describe the significance of training records in GMP as per Schedule T.
11. What are the main objectives of Schedule T - GMP?
12. Explain the importance of warehousing in GMP as per Schedule T.
13. How does Schedule T ensure the safety of herbal products in terms of raw materials?
14. What are the guidelines related to the personnel's health and hygiene in Schedule T?
15. Describe the importance of documentation in GMP as per Schedule T.
16. Why is the logical flow of working space essential in GMP?
17. How do regulatory hurdles challenge the herbal drugs industry?
18. Describe the role of the Central Institute of Medicinal and Aromatic Plants (CIMAP) in India.
19. What is the significance of the "Location" component in Schedule T's GMP?
20. How do SOPs contribute to the consistency of operations in GMP?

Long Answer Type Questions (Subjective)

1. Elaborate on the present scope of the herbal drugs industry and highlight its significance in global healthcare.
2. Discuss the future prospects of the herbal drugs industry and explain how technological advancements might reshape it.
3. Provide a comprehensive overview of the challenges faced by the herbal drugs industry and suggest potential solutions to address them.
4. Describe the role and contributions of prominent plant-based industries and institutions in promoting medicinal and aromatic plants in India.
5. Elaborate on the objectives of Schedule T - GMP and explain its significance in ensuring the quality and safety of ASU medicines.
6. Discuss the infrastructural requirements as per Schedule T and explain their importance in maintaining the quality of ASU medicines.
7. Provide a detailed overview of the machinery and equipment's requirements as per Schedule T and their role in ensuring the consistent quality of products.
8. Describe the importance of standard operating procedures (SOPs) in GMP as per Schedule T and explain their role in maintaining product quality and safety.
9. Discuss the significance of health and hygiene requirements in GMP as per Schedule T and explain their role in ensuring product safety.
10. Elaborate on the importance of documentation and record-keeping in GMP as per Schedule T and explain their role in ensuring product quality and traceability.

Answer Key for MCQs

1. (c) Asia, Africa, and Latin America
2. (c) Herbal formulations
3. (c) Standardization and Quality Control

4. (c) Increasing consumer preference for natural products
5. (b) Enhanced production of therapeutic phytochemicals
6. (c) They consist of complex mixtures
7. (b) Johnson & Johnson
8. (b) Central Institute of Medicinal and Aromatic Plants
9. (c) Good Manufacturing Practices for ASU medicines
10.(b) Marketing strategies
11.(b) To provide a blueprint for the production of each product
12.(b) Contagious diseases
13.(c) Made of corrosion-resistant material
14.(c) They should maintain a high degree of personal cleanliness
15.(b) Significant attention worldwide
16.(c) Designated authority
17.(b) Ensuring processes are consistent and can be audited
18.(c) Nanotechnology
19.(b) Conservation of medicinal plants and biodiversity
20.(c) Kerala

www.ingramcontent.com/pod-product-compliance
Lightning Source LLC
LaVergne TN
LVHW021136160826
845679LV00023B/1924

* 9 7 9 8 8 9 4 1 5 8 1 7 4 *